ROUTLEDGE LIBRARY EDITIONS:
18TH CENTURY PHILOSOPHY

Volume 6

HUME'S SKEPTICISM IN THE TREATISE OF HUMAN NATURE

HUME'S SKEPTICISM IN THE TREATISE OF HUMAN NATURE

ROBERT J. FOGELIN

LONDON AND NEW YORK

First published in 1985 by Routledge & Kegan Paul plc

This edition first published in 2019
by Routledge
2 Park Square, Milton Park, Abingdon, Oxon OX14 4RN

and by Routledge
52 Vanderbilt Avenue, New York, NY 10017

Routledge is an imprint of the Taylor & Francis Group, an informa business

© 1985 Robert J. Fogelin

All rights reserved. No part of this book may be reprinted or reproduced or utilised in any form or by any electronic, mechanical, or other means, now known or hereafter invented, including photocopying and recording, or in any information storage or retrieval system, without permission in writing from the publishers.

Trademark notice: Product or corporate names may be trademarks or registered trademarks, and are used only for identification and explanation without intent to infringe.

British Library Cataloguing in Publication Data
A catalogue record for this book is available from the British Library

ISBN: 978-0-367-13518-8 (Set)
ISBN: 978-0-429-02691-1 (Set) (ebk)
ISBN: 978-0-367-18371-4 (Volume 6) (hbk)
ISBN: 978-0-367-18372-1 (Volume 6) (pbk)
ISBN: 978-0-429-06116-5 (Volume 6) (ebk)

Publisher's Note
The publisher has gone to great lengths to ensure the quality of this reprint but points out that some imperfections in the original copies may be apparent.

Disclaimer
The publisher has made every effort to trace copyright holders and would welcome correspondence from those they have been unable to trace.

Hume's Skepticism in the
Treatise of Human Nature

Robert J. Fogelin

ROUTLEDGE & KEGAN PAUL
London, Boston, Melbourne and Henley

*First published in 1985
by Routledge & Kegan Paul plc*

14 Leicester Square, London WC2H 7PH, England

9 Park Street, Boston, Mass. 02108, USA

*464 St Kilda Road, Melbourne,
Victoria 3004, Australia and*

*Broadway House, Newtown Road,
Henley-on-Thames, Oxon RG9 1EN, England*

*Set in Linotron Times
by Input Typesetting Ltd, London
and printed in Great Britain
by St Edmundsbury Press Ltd,
Bury St Edmunds, Suffolk*

Copyright © Robert J. Fogelin 1985

*No part of this book may be reproduced in
any form without permission from the publisher,
except for the quotation of brief passages
in criticism*

Library of Congress Cataloging in Publication Data

Fogelin, Robert J.
Hume's skepticism in the Treatise of Human Nature.
(International library of philosophy)
Bibliography: p.
Includes index.
1. Hume, David, 1711–1776. Treatise of Human Nature.
2. Skepticism. 3. Knowledge, Theory of.
I. Title. II. Series.
B1489.F64   1985   128   84–15101

British Library CIP data also available

ISBN 0–7102–0368–3(c)

For
W. T. J. and M. O. B.

LADY BRUTE: I think, sir, your sophistry
has all the effect you can reasonably expect
it should have: it puzzles, but don't convince.

The Provok'd Wife
John Vanbrugh

CONTENTS

	Texts and Citations	ix
	Preface	xi
	Introduction	1
I	Aspects of Hume's Skepticism	5
II	Hume's Skepticism Concerning Reason	13
III	Hume's Answer to Bayle's Skepticism Concerning Extension	25
IV	Causality, Necessity, and Induction	38
V	Skepticism and the Triumph of the Imagination	53
VI	Skepticism with Regard to the Senses	64
VII	Hume's Natural History of Philosophy	80
VIII	The Soul and the Self	93
IX	Reason and the Passions	109
X	Reason and Morals	123

Contents

XI	Conclusion	146

Appendix A Interpretations and Criticisms of Hume's Inductive Skepticism 152

Appendix B Hume's Regularity Definition of Causation 167

    Notes 172

    Bibliography 186

    Index 192

TEXTS AND CITATIONS

All citations to *A Treatise of Human Nature* and the *Abstract* are to the second Selby-Bigge edition, revised with notes by P. H. Nidditch. Only the page numbers are given. Citations to *An Enquiry Concerning Human Understanding* are to the third Selby-Bigge edition of Hume's two *Enquiries*, revised with notes by P. H. Nidditch. They read *E.* followed by the page reference. All other citations are in standard footnote form. *G and G* is an abbreviation for *David Hume: The Philosophical Works*, edited by Green and Grose.

PREFACE

This work offers a general interpretation of Hume's *Treatise of Human Nature* written, as my friend Michael Williams remarked, to commemorate the 207th anniversary of its author's death. I am aware that a more notable anniversary has brought forth a great deal of writing on Hume's philosophy and that much of it is excellent. Even setting aside this recent outburst, it cannot be said that Hume's philosophy has suffered neglect during the middle portion of this century. Indeed, Hume scholarship has been blessed with commentators who combine historical knowledge with philosophical ability.

The robust state of Hume scholarship raises a question and poses a problem. The question, of course, is why another book on Hume, in particular, why another *general* book on Hume? My answer is that most recent Hume scholarship has either neglected or downplayed an important aspect of Hume's position – his skepticism – and this needs putting right. The problem, which faces anyone who writes a broad work on Hume's philosophy, is to find some way to acknowledge debts to others. I know, for example, the book that has influenced me most: it is John Passmore's *Hume's Intentions*. It has corrected my thoughts both at large and in detail, yet it is often difficult to say just how without entering into a complex second-order discussion comparing what Hume says with what Passmore says with what I say. In any case, students of Hume will recognize my debt to Passmore and I wish to acknowledge it. I have also found two other recent works on Hume's general philosophy particularly useful. They both bear

Preface

the title *Hume*: one was written by Terence Penelhum, the other by Barry Stroud.

One way that this work differs from the three just mentioned is that it gives more prominence to Hume's skepticism than they do. I first became interested in skeptical arguments through conversations with Richard Popkin held, appropriately enough, over a pool table. Popkin convinced me that a patronizing and dismissive attitude toward skeptical arguments is antithetical to a sympathetic and just reading of much early modern philosophy including the philosophy of David Hume. Without saddling Popkin with many of the things that I say about Hume's skepticism, I wish to acknowledge that debt as well.

I have also learned a great deal from interpreters of Hume with whom I disagree. Here I should mention D. C. Stove and J. L. Mackie. I think that they both misrepresent the structure of Hume's argument for inductive skepticism, but their interpretations are at least plausible, and have lifted the level of debate on this issue. On other matters I have learned a great deal from them.

My deepest disagreements are with Norman Kemp Smith and those who have followed him in giving what I take to be a one-sided emphasis to Hume's naturalism at the expense of his skepticism. In many ways this work is a response to them. However, in the body of the text, I have only rarely discussed competing interpretations directly, reserving most criticism (and acknowledgment) for the footnotes and the two appendices that close this work.

Florence Fogelin and Teri Allbright helped edit the manuscript, and the costs of preparation were supported by the Griswold Fund, administered by the Humanities Division of Yale University, and by the Research Committee of Dartmouth College.

INTRODUCTION

> If we try to show that Hume is really a phenomenalist, or a skeptic, or a naturalist, and that those sections of his work which will not fit into such a single philosophical system are no more than slips of the pen, we shall have to admit that his "slips" are of gigantic proportions; and we shall be quite baffled by the way in which he not merely falls into, but goes out of his way to develop and extol, views which are quite incompatible with whatever systematic doctrine we care to ascribe to him. John Passmore[1]

It is now possible to write about Hume's philosophy without including a preliminary denunciation of the "traditional" idea that Hume's contribution to philosophy was to work out the skeptical consequences inherent in British Empiricism. Though a slight exaggeration, it is more correct to say that he did *nothing* of the kind. A scholarly consensus has emerged that Hume's primary intentions (and achievements) were constructive. His aim was to develop a Science of Man through introducing "the experimental method of reasoning into moral subjects."

But accepting this new dispensation does not solve all the problems of Hume scholarship, and insisting upon it in a heavy-handed way can itself lead to distortions and misrepresentations of the text. In particular, many of Hume's naturalistic interpreters now undervalue the skeptical dimensions of his position, for once it is decided that Hume's aim was not to unfold the skeptical

Introduction

consequences of British Empiricism, skepticism itself is given low priority in the general interpretation of Hume's philosophy.

Yet the *Treatise* is packed with skeptical arguments. The first book contains skeptical arguments aimed, in turn, at the *understanding*, *reason*, and the *senses*. Book III, which concerns morals, contains a skeptical argument that shows deep similarities to the skepticism of Book I. Book II is about the passions – not a natural topic for skeptical attack – but even here Hume finds arguments intended to curb the pretensions of reason. These skeptical arguments are embedded in a naturalistic program intended to offer causal explanations of mental phenomena. Understanding the relationship between these skeptical arguments and Hume's naturalistic program is one of the central problems for interpreting the *Treatise* as a whole.

We should notice from the start that the degree of Hume's skeptical commitment is variable – and, as we shall see, there are good reasons for this. His general posture is that of a moderate skeptic recommending that we modestly restrict our inquiries to topics within our ken and, recognizing our fallibility, adjust our beliefs to probabilities. For Hume this diffidence is essential for scientific inquiry, but it is also appropriate for a "man of letters," since it may help curb superstition and enthusiasm. Now this moderate – probabilistic, academic – skepticism raises few problems for the general interpretation of Hume's philosophy; indeed, it complements Hume's overall naturalistic program. But in his closet, Hume traffics in a more radical version of skepticism that is Pyrrhonian rather than Carneadean. It is these strong skeptical arguments that lend excitement to Hume's early writings. At the same time, these arguments raise problems of interpretation, for Pyrrhonism, let loose, threatens to destroy everything, including itself. More specifically, then, this work is an attempt to understand the relationship between Hume's *radical* skepticism and his naturalism.

What about Hume's empiricism? Strange to say, this seems to be the least understood aspect of his philosophy. The fault, however, lies with Hume himself. It may be hard to believe that a philosopher of Hume's critical ability could have developed this side of his philosophy in such a casual, careless, and inconsistent manner – all the time trumpeting its importance. Yet a close reading of the text can lead to no other conclusion. The best

Introduction

reason for rejecting the idea that Hume thought *out* the skeptical consequences inherent in British Empiricism is that he hardly seems to have thought *about* the foundations of this viewpoint at all.

All the same, empiricism (sometimes tending to a phenomenalism) plays an important role in various parts of the text and its significance must be understood as well. It is not, however, always easy to identify arguments that proceed from his empiricist commitments, for there are times when the empiricist language is simply window dressing and can be replaced, without argumentative loss, by a neutral reference to objects or things. (In fact, Hume often drops the official empiricist language in just this way.) That many of Hume's important arguments will tolerate translation into a neutral idiom may explain, in part at least, the staying power of his thought. At other times, the empiricist standpoint serves as a reasonable (though not forced) foundation for Hume's naturalistic program. Laws of Association do not have to be applied to ideas – they can also be applied to dispositions – yet ideas are natural candidates to be the subject of associational laws. Hume's causal accounts of mental phenomena are largely, though not exclusively, developed on this basis. Finally, at various places in the *Treatise*, empiricist commitments or, more generally, commitments to the way of ideas, play a substantive role in the development of the argument. This occurs, for example, in the complex discussion *Of Scepticism with Regard to the Senses*. There, I shall argue, Hume pays the price for his uncritical acceptance and incoherent development of the empiricist framework.

I should say a few words about the scope of this work. It concerns the *Treatise* and makes no important claims about Hume's other works. Thus when I speak of Hume's philosophy, I mean, unless the context clearly indicates otherwise, Hume's philosophy as expressed in that work. In fact, I do not think that Hume ever abandoned the skeptical standpoint expressed in the *Treatise*, and thus I disagree with those who detect a fundamental shift in skeptical commitments in *An Enquiry Concerning Human Understanding*. I shall not defend that thesis here,[2] but I shall not rely on it either. On those occasions where I cite the *Enquiry*, it is only because the phrasing in some passage is more apt or striking than the corresponding passage in the *Treatise*. The only place that I have made extensive reference outside the *Treatise* is

Introduction

in the discussion of passions and morals. There I have cited various essays published in the second volume of Hume's *Essays, Moral and Political*. These essays appeared in 1742, only four years after the publication of the *Treatise*, and are written thoroughly in its spirit. I defend this claim at the one place it may seem dubious.

Since I believe that most recent interpretations of Hume's philosophy have tended to underplay the systematic importance of his skepticism, I have chosen to begin with this topic. As the work continues, naturalistic themes come more into prominence.

I

ASPECTS OF HUME'S SKEPTICISM

This discussion of Hume's skepticism will turn upon a series of contrasts – contrasts that cut across each other in various ways: (i) Theoretical vs prescriptive skepticism, (ii) Antecedent vs consequent skepticism, and (iii) Epistemological vs conceptual skepticism. Before turning to the text, let me explain what I mean by these contrasts.

(i) *Theoretical vs prescriptive skepticism*. Quite simply, a theoretical skeptic calls into question the supposed *grounds* or *warrant* for some system of beliefs. A radical skeptic will argue that the challenged system of beliefs is wholly ungrounded, whereas a more moderate skeptic will argue that the beliefs in question are less well-grounded than commonly thought. A prescriptive skeptic (perhaps on the basis of theoretical skepticism) calls for a suspension of belief or, more moderately, calls for more caution in giving assent than is common. A practicing skeptic is one who follows or adheres to such prescriptions. Clearly, a philosopher can be a theoretical skeptic of the most general and radical kind without prescribing anything about holding beliefs and without himself following any such prescriptions. This distinction, though obvious enough, is important, for it disposes at once of vulgar *ad hominem* arguments that attempt to refute the skeptic by pointing to his conduct which, it is said, gives the lie to his supposed skepticism.[1]

(ii) *Antecedent vs consequent skepticism*. The distinction between antecedent and consequent skepticism is provided by Hume himself in *An Enquiry Concerning Human Understanding*. There he speaks of a

Aspects of Hume's Skepticism

species of scepticism, *antecedent* to all study and philosophy
. . . [which] . . . recommends an universal doubt, not only of
all our former opinions and principles, but also of our very
faculties; of whose veracity, say they, we must assure
ourselves, by a chain of reasoning, deduced from some original
principle, which cannot possibly be fallacious or deceitful.
(*E*. pp. 149–50)

He contrasts this with "another species of scepticism, *consequent* to science and enquiry, when men are supposed to have discovered, either the absolute fallaciousness of their mental faculties, or their unfitness to reach any fixed determination in all those curious subjects of speculation, about which they are commonly employed" (*E*. p. 150). Analogically, a person who refuses to accept political authority until its credentials have been established, is an antecedent skeptic; one who abandons his belief in political authority, having discovered the corruption and venality of political institutions, is a consequent skeptic.

(iii) *Epistemological vs conceptual skepticism*. This distinction cuts along different lines than those just mentioned. An epistemological skeptic accepts a system of beliefs as intelligible, but challenges the supposed grounds for these beliefs. A conceptual skeptic challenges the very intelligibility of a system of beliefs. Hume's skepticism concerning induction is an example of an epistemological skepticism, for he holds that we have no rational grounds to support our inductive inferences. He does not, however, suggest that our inductive inferences make no sense. By way of contrast, Bayle's argument that the idea of extension is unintelligible is, as we shall see,[2] an example of conceptual skepticism. The first book of Bradley's *Appearance and Reality* is a compendium of such conceptually skeptical arguments. The lasting fame of the logical positivist movement lies primarily in trafficking in such arguments.

With these contrasts in hand, I can state the fundamental theses of this work. (i) Hume accepts a theoretical epistemological skepticism that is wholly unmitigated. Nothing except the immediate contents of sense is immune to this skepticism. (ii) In contrast, Hume's prescriptive skepticism is carefully circumscribed. Given his theory of belief, it is not in our power to suspend belief by a simple act of the mind. Our beliefs are causally determined, and

Aspects of Hume's Skepticism

our choices are not determinants of these beliefs. Hume calls for (or attempts to induce) a suspension of belief only for those reflections that go beyond our natural capacities. Such beliefs, when formed, can be undermined by skeptical arguments and, more importantly, they are not reinstated by the influence of everyday life. (iii) Hume's attitude toward antecedent as opposed to consequent skepticism is more problematic, and can only be examined adequately with respect to particular texts. Very broadly, to the extent that Hume invokes standard *a priori* skeptical arguments (involving infinite regress, circularity, etc.) his skepticism has an antecedent (or Cartesian) character. His skepticism with regard to reason and his skepticism with regard to induction seem to fall into this category. In contrast, to the extent that his arguments turn upon empirical discoveries concerning the nature of our mental faculties, his skepticism is of a consequent kind. His skepticism concerning the senses and his skepticism concerning morality have this character.

(iv) It is not easy to assess the extent of Hume's conceptual skepticism. Looking back from the perspective of the twentieth century there is a strong temptation to place Hume at the head of the logical positivist tradition – a view, by the way, shared both by the positivists and their critics.[3] Without denying the existence of positivistic themes in Hume's philosophy, my own inclination is to minimize them. Hume's fundamental task is to provide a naturalistic account of the origin of ideas and the belief that we reside in them, and conceptual skepticism, in denying that a term has any coherent idea corresponding to it, thwarts this investigation. In particular, I do not think that Hume is a conceptual skeptic concerning any of the concepts that arise in daily life. Hume will often argue that the plain man is deeply mistaken concerning the true nature of the ideas that correspond to the terms that he uses, but he does not argue that the plain man uses terms that lack a corresponding idea. To the extent that it exists, Hume's conceptual skepticism seems to be limited to philosophical conceits – the Idols of the Theatre. He does hold, quite explicitly, that the word "vacuum," as philosophers use it, has no idea corresponding to it (pp. 53ff.). A similar case can be made for his treatment of the ancient philosopher's notions of *substance* and *attribute* and the modern philosopher's distinction between *primary* and *secondary qualities*.

Aspects of Hume's Skepticism

More generally, I do not think that it is characteristic of Hume's philosophy, as it was of the philosophy of the logical positivists, to proceed from a criterion of meaningfulness, and evaluate philosophical positions in terms of it. Since this is a controversial claim, and not one that I shall consider in detail again, it might be useful to defend it from the start.

Perhaps the most positivistic passage in Hume's writings appears as the ringing conclusion to the *Enquiry*:

> If we take in our hand any volume; of divinity or school metaphysics, for instance; let us ask, *Does it contain any abstract reasoning concerning quantity or number?* No. *Does it contain any experimental reasoning concerning matter of fact and existence?* No. Commit it then to the flames: for it can contain nothing but sophistry and illusion. (*E*. p. 165)[4]

Hume's language here could not be more deprecatory, but is he claiming that the pronouncements of divinity and school metaphysics are literally meaningless? I think not. I see no hidden irony in the following passage that also occurs on the final page of the *Enquiry*:

> Divinity or Theology, as it proves the existence of a Deity, and the immortality of souls, is composed partly of reasonings concerning particular, partly concerning general facts. It has a foundation in *reason*, so far as it is supported by experience. But its best and most solid foundation is *faith* and divine revelation. (*E*. p. 165)

Skeptical philosophy may deprive Divinity and Theology of their *proofs*, but it does not deprive them of the objects of these proofs. For Hume, the concept of God is sufficiently intelligible to allow us to ask whether proofs for his/her existence are any good.

Again, if we search Hume's *Dialogues Concerning Natural Religion* for positivistic arguments, we will be disappointed. The central argument of that work is evidential: given a relatively well defined notion of a deity, Cleanthes and Philo dispute the degree of support empirical arguments give for the existence of such an entity. The ostensible (and I think real) conclusion of this work is that the evidence for the existence of anything like a traditional deity is negligible. There is no suggestion that the notion of such a deity is unintelligible. Similarly, Hume's *Natural History of Reli-*

Aspects of Hume's Skepticism

gion is an attempt to give a naturalistic account of the origins and developments of man's ideas of a deity. This enterprise would be peculiarly out of focus if Hume held that there is no idea corresponding to this word. Hume often treats religious beliefs with contempt, for as a potential source of *enthusiasm* they can be dangerous. He never suggests, as the positivists have, that they are non-beliefs or pseudo-beliefs.

Turning to the *Treatise*, we can raise this question in a more systematic way by searching the text for remarks that seem to express an empiricist criterion of meaning. I think that Hume comes closest to laying down such a criterion in the following passage:

> No discovery cou'd have been made more happily for deciding all controversies concerning ideas, than . . . that impressions always take the precedency of them, and that every idea, with which the imagination is furnish'd, first makes its appearance in a correspondent impression. These latter perceptions are all so clear and evident, that they admit of no controversy; tho' many of our ideas are so obscure, that 'tis almost impossible even for the mind, which forms them, to tell exactly their nature and composition. (p. 33)

Now as it stands, this passage does not lay down a criterion of meaning; instead, it specifies a method for *making our ideas clear*. This is precisely how Hume claims to use it in the discussion of space and time – the context in which the passage appears.

hume quotes this passage in the *Abstract* and, affecting the third person, comments on it in these words:

> Accordingly, whenever any idea is ambiguous he has always recourse to the impression which must render it clear and precise. (p. 648)

Here it is an *idea*, not a *term*, that is said to be ambiguous. We get some idea of what Hume means by calling an idea ambiguous by noticing the contrasting expressions "clear and precise." But this passage from the *Abstract* continues in a way that is as positivistic as one could want:

> And when he suspects that any philosophical term has no idea annexed to it (as is too common), he always asks *from what*

> *impression that pretended idea is derived?* And if no impression can be produced, he concludes that the term is altogether insignificant. 'Tis after this manner he examines our idea of *substance* and *essence*; and it were to be wished, that this rigorous method were practised in all philosophical debates. (pp. 648–9)

This is clear enough: when we believe, quite mistakenly, that an idea corresponds to some term, then the search for the appropriate impressions can show this. Thus the passage unequivocally lays down a criterion of meaningfulness. Our question, then, is whether this appeal to impressions to determine the meaningfulness of a term or the earlier appeal to clarify the nature of an idea predominates in the text. Without denying the occurrence of postivistic episodes in the text, it seems to me that the appeal to impressions is used primarily for the analysis of ideas and only secondarily to show that words are sometimes used without meaning.

Consider the reference to *substance* in the passage just cited. It may seem that Hume is saying that the term "substance" has no idea annexed to it; indeed, the passage seems to admit of no other reading. Yet an examination of the *Treatise* shows that Hume's position is more complex than this. He discusses substance in two main places in the text.[5] In Book I, Part I, Section VI he examines the distinction between substances and modes, i.e., the common distinction between an individual and its properties. He asks whether the idea of a substance "be deriv'd from the impressions of sensation or reflexion" (pp. 15–16) and immediately denies that it arises from either of these two sources. Since the division is, for Hume, exhaustive, we might expect, in line with the passage just cited from the *Abstract*, that he will say that there is no idea annexed to this word at all. Here is what he says instead:

> We have therefore no idea of substance, distinct from that of a collection of particular qualities, nor have we any other meaning when we either talk or reason concerning it. (p. 16)

Hume does not say, as a positivist might, that we have no idea at all of substance. More carefully, he has shown to his satisfaction that we have no *simple* idea of substance, for he defines a substance as a particular kind of complex idea:

Aspects of Hume's Skepticism

> The idea of substance . . . is nothing but a collection of simple ideas, that are united by the imagination, and have a particular name assigned to them, by which we are able to recall, either to ourselves or others, that collection. (p. 16)

Thus with respect to the commonsense notion of an individual thing in contrast with its properties or modes, Hume is not a conceptual skeptic. Of course, the plain man does not realize that the unity of individual things is the product of his imagination, indeed, he would deny this. It remains a fact, however, that there is a proper idea annexed to the notion of an individual substance.

Hume's attitude toward the *philosopher's* use of the notion of substance is different and less charitable, and here a case can be made that his philosophy employs something like an empiricist criterion of meaning. In his discussion of the ancient philosophy, he speaks of the "unintelligible chimera of a substance" (p. 222). Now on the face of it, the notion of an unintelligible chimera does not make sense. There is nothing unintelligible about a mythical beast and if something is unintelligible then it isn't so much as a mythical beast. Quite simply, if a word has any sort of idea attached to it, then it is intelligible, for, on Hume's own theory, there could be no such thing as an unintelligible idea. So what Hume must mean when he speaks of substance as an unintelligible chimera, is that the word "substance" has no idea associated with it. This, in fact, is what he says. Concerning views of substance, there are, he tells us,

> three opinions, that rise above each other, according as the persons, who form them, acquire new degrees of reason and knowledge. These opinions are that of the vulgar, that of a false philosophy, and that of the true; . . . (p. 222)

As we have already seen, the vulgar, under the influence of the imagination, falsely attribute genuine connections to the various qualities of an object. The false philosopher, as the result of a little learning, detects this error in the plain man's views, and then tries to preserve the core of the vulgar view by presenting the surrogate notion of an underlying substance.[6] True philosophy detects this sham and returns to the view of the vulgar even while recognizing, abstractly, at least, that it is literally false.

But a puzzle still remains: what is the content of the false

Aspects of Hume's Skepticism

philosopher's belief in substance? Hume's answer seems to be that it is contentless, but then what does the belief amount to? Hume's ingenious answer takes the following form:

> But as nature seems to have observ'd a kind of justice and compensation in every thing, she has not neglected philosophers more than the rest of the creation; but has reserv'd them a consolation amid all their disappointments and afflictions. This consolation principally consists in their invention of . . . words . . . (p. 224)

Having invented words to cover their embarrassment, philosophers then proceed to use them in ways similar to the use of ordinary words:

> so it naturally happens, that after the frequent use of terms, which are wholly insignificant and unintelligible, we fancy them to be on the same footing with [meaningful terms], and to have a secret meaning, which we might discover by reflection. . . . By this means these philosophers set themselves at ease, and arrive at last, by an illusion, at the same indifference, which people attain by their stupidity, and true philosophers by their moderate scepticism. (p. 224)

Of course, the people's stupidity involves an illusion too – the illusion of a connectedness between qualities that does not exist – but the philosopher suffers from an illusion of a more radical kind: the illusion of intelligibility where there is none.

In anticipation of detailed discussions that will come later, the extent of Hume's conceptual skepticism amounts to this. With respect to common non-philosophical beliefs, Hume holds that they are sometimes unfounded, often false, and characteristically involve fictions. They are not, however, unintelligible. Unintelligibility emerges when the philosopher, in the throes of partial insight, falls back on empty verbiage in his attempts to find a surrogate for the views he has rejected but still cannot abandon.

II

HUME'S SKEPTICISM CONCERNING REASON

The first book of the *Treatise* contains three famous skeptical arguments yielding: (i) a skepticism concerning induction, (ii) a skepticism with regard to reason, and (iii) a skepticism with regard to the senses. The first and third arguments apply to a large yet limited domain. The skepticism concerning induction calls into question *all* inferences from present and past experience to other experience (most notably to future experience). I shall examine this argument in detail later on, but for our present purposes it is sufficient to notice that Hume *intends* his skepticism to be wholly unmitigated within its range of application. Every inference from what is present to what is not present is on a par in having no rational foundation. Hume's skepticism with regard to the senses is more deeply entrenched in the special features of his position. Roughly speaking, given his account of experience, he calls into question those arguments intended to show that objects we are aware of can have a continued and distinct existence. Once more, the skeptical argument has a limited domain of application, yet it is wholly unmitigated within this domain.

I have chosen to look first at Hume's skepticism with regard to reason, for this argument, more than any other, reveals Hume's intentions.[1] In one way, this skeptical argument is on a par with the two skeptical arguments just noticed. Surveying the faculties of the human mind, Hume raises skeptical doubts concerning the *understanding*, skeptical doubts concerning the *senses*, and here he raises skeptical doubts concerning *reason*. There is, however, an important difference between this skeptical argument and the

Hume's Skepticism Concerning Reason

previous two. Although it is aimed at a particular target – our demonstrative reasoning – in effect its range of application is wholly unrestricted. This is shown by the structure of the argument, which has two main steps: (i) the reduction of knowledge to probability, and (ii) the reduction of any assigned probability, as he says, "to nothing." The purpose of the first step is to make knowledge subject to the argument given in the second step. The second step applies to all probable reasoning whatsoever. Thus if we begin with a distinction between knowledge and probability, reduce the first to the second, and then argue that, upon reflection, all probabilities must be reduced "to nothing," we arrive at a skepticism unlimited in its application and wholly unmitigated. We arrive at a *general* skepticism on a par, in its way, with the Pyrrhonian argument from the criterion of truth.[2]

(i) The first step in Hume's argument – the reduction of knowledge to probability – itself falls into two parts. When Hume first speaks about *knowledge*, he divides it into two categories: *intuition* and *demonstration* (p. 70). Since his aim is to reduce all knowledge to probability, his argument will be incomplete if intuitive knowledge is left untouched. Since his central argument is aimed at *all* the products of reason, he begins by rejecting a sharp distinction between intuition and demonstration. This, I think, is the point of the following line of reasoning that uses arithmetic truths as an example:

> Now as none will maintain, that our assurance in a long numeration exceeds probability, I may safely affirm, that there scarce is any proposition concerning numbers, of which we can have a fuller security. For 'tis easily possible, by gradually diminishing the numbers, to reduce the longest series of addition to the most simple question, which can be form'd, to an addition of two single numbers; and upon this supposition we shall find it impracticable to shew the precise limits of knowledge and of probability, or discover that particular number, at which the one ends and the other begins. But knowledge and probability are of such contrary and disagreeing natures, that they cannot well run insensibly into each other, and that because they will not divide, but must be either entirely present, or entirely absent. Besides, if any single addition were certain, every one wou'd be so,

Hume's Skepticism Concerning Reason

and consequently the whole or total sum; unless the whole
can be different from all its parts. I had almost said, that this
was certain; but I reflect, that it must reduce *itself*, as well
as every other reasoning, and from knowledge degenerate into
probability. (p. 181)

Although the example concerns arithmetic, the closing sentence – with its important self-referential twist – gives the argument full application to all knowledge claims.

We can notice that this argument assumes that a long addition can only yield probability. (I shall examine Hume's argument for that claim next.) Then, by slippery slope argument (run in two directions), Hume argues that this must be true of any addition however simple. The reply, of course, is that this ignores the possibility that our grasp of a simple "proposition concerning numbers" may not involve calculation at all but, instead, an immediate insight. In this way, the fallibility that infects our calculations (and demonstrations) need not touch our intuitive understanding. Nonetheless, by this argument Hume intends to show that the probability of error which (as no one denies) infects large computations must to some degree infect our beliefs in the most simple mathematical propositions.

Hume's next move in this part of his argument may be no more persuasive than the last, but it is revelatory of his fundamental approach to philosophical problems. He immediately offers a *causal* account of this liability of the human mind to fall into error in its demonstrative reasoning:

Our reason must be consider'd as a kind of cause, of which
truth is the natural effect; but such-a-one as by the irruption
of other causes, and by the inconsistency of our mental powers,
may frequently be prevented. (p. 180)

Here Hume's naturalistic conception of the mind is carried to the seat of reason. In a more famous part of the *Treatise*, Hume argues that our *causal* inferences have no rational foundation; instead, they derive from a natural (or animal) propensity of the mind to project past regularities into the future. The plain suggestion of this passage is that reasoning itself is another natural propensity. Presented with certain ideas, the mind is naturally

Hume's Skepticism Concerning Reason

led to believe that certain relations obtain among them. Hume's naturalism runs very deep.

At this point, the form of Hume's skeptical argument becomes clear: if reason "must be considered as a kind of cause," then the canons of *causal* reason apply to it. It is a general fact about causal relations that they obtain only under special circumstances. A may normally cause B, but with "an irruption of other causes" that alters the normal situation, A may occur without being followed by B. From these reflections, Hume immediately concludes that:

> By these means all knowledge degenerates into probability; and this probability is greater or less, according to our experience of the veracity or deceitfulness of our understanding, and according to the simplicity or intricacy of the question. (p. 180)

In the final clause of this passage, Hume acknowledges that we are less likely to go wrong on simple questions, but he insists that there is still some probability (however slight) that a mistake has been made.

The force of Hume's argument can now be stated in two propositions, one prescriptive, the other theoretical:

> [1] "In every judgment, which we can form concerning probability, as well as concerning knowledge, we ought always to correct the first judgment, deriv'd from the nature of the object, by another judgment, deriv'd from the nature of the understanding." (pp. 181–2)

> [2] Given the natural fallibility of judgment, this probability must always fall short of certainty.[3]

In the end, Hume abandons this first (prescriptive) principle, but only after his skeptical argument is fully developed.

(ii) The second step in Hume's argument – the reduction of all probability "to nothing" – is a morass. Suppose we have made the first two steps outlined above, that is, we have formed a particular judgment (in a natural way) and then considered the probability that in this case our faculties have erred. Now, according to Hume:

> we are oblig'd by our reason to add a new doubt deriv'd from

Hume's Skepticism Concerning Reason

the possibility of error in the estimation we make of the truth and fidelity of our faculties. This is a doubt, which immediately occurs to us, and of which, if we wou'd closely pursue our reason, we cannot avoid giving a decision. But this decision, tho' it shou'd be favourable to our preceeding judgment, being founded only on probability, must weaken still further our first evidence, and must itself be weaken'd by a fourth doubt of the same kind, and so on *in infinitum*; till at last there remain nothing of the original probability, however great we may suppose it to have been, and however small the diminution by every new uncertainty. No finite object can subsist under a decrease repeated *in infinitum*; and even the vastest quantity, which can enter into human imagination, must in this manner be reduc'd to nothing. (p. 182)

So Hume concludes that "all the rules of logic require a continual diminution, and at last a total extinction of belief and evidence" (p. 183).

Let me comment briefly on the soundness of this argument. If we *provisionally* grant the general form of the argument, we can still notice that an important step is missing. In order for the diminutions, however small, to decrease a quantity "to nothing," it must be shown that those diminutions do not approach zero as a limit. That is, we can imagine each diminution becoming progressively smaller such that the sum of the diminution approaches a finite limit.[4] The total diminution could even be quite small. Hume does not anticipate this objection (and, in general, he has a bad head for questions concerning infinity), but we can imagine what he could say in reply. He need only argue that there is some finite degree of probability below which the chance of error never falls. (We might call a minimal residue of doubt a niggle.) For example, however careful we are, there is always 1 chance in $10^{10000000}$ that we have made a mistake. Given a suitably large number, this reply does not seem implausible. But more to the point, we will be in a perilous state if our only reply to Hume's argument depends upon rejecting any such minimal degree of possible error.

We can get a better grasp of Hume's argument – and thus see what is wrong with it – by asking the following question: exactly how does the diminution in probability take place? Suppose we

Hume's Skepticism Concerning Reason

consider the claim that one plus one equals two. We can further suppose that reason naturally accepts this claim, assigning to it the probability 1. More carefully, given the kind of proposition it is, we must assign to it either the probability 1 or the probability 0, and reason leads us to make the assignment 1. Even so, we might wonder whether we are correct in assigning the probability 1 rather than the probability 0. We now have a new claim to consider:

> I am correct in assigning the probability of 1 to the proposition one plus one equals two.

This, if Hume is correct, is a probabilistic judgment, and the degree of probability that we will assign to it depends upon our assessment of the reliability of our faculties to deal with such matters. We might maintain that here the probability is extraordinarily high, but this concedes Hume's point. However high it is, it does not amount to certainty.

Hume's next point is that these considerations must lead us to lower the probability assignment given to the original proposition. This, however, is simply wrong. However certain or uncertain we are about our ability to calculate probabilities, if a proposition has a certain probability, that (tautologically) is the probability it has. For example, in a complex case we may be uncertain whether to assign the probability 1 or 0 to a mathematical proposition, yet this does not affect the first-level probability assignment, giving it some intermediate value.

I know that some will quarrel with the above argument on the grounds that it takes advantage of the fact that it is not possible to assign some value between 1 and 0 to mathematical propositions. (More reasonably, it might be suggested that it makes no sense to assign *any* probability value to a mathematical proposition.) But even if we grant the force of this objection, it does not change the argument in any substantial way. Suppose, on the basis of certain evidence, we assign a probability of 0.8 to a given proposition. Then, following Hume's instructions, we reflect upon our ability to make such probability assignments. We might recognize that we are not very good at this sort of thing and assign a probability of 0.5 to the proposition that our original assignment was correct. Does this, in any way, alter the probability of the original proposition? Again the answer is no.

Hume's Skepticism Concerning Reason

Finally we can consider a more sophisticated version of Hume's argument. We may grant that our higher-level fallibility will not change the first level probability from, say, 0.8 to 0.7, but perhaps it should lead us to make the weaker claim that the probability falls within a range of values clustering around 0.8. Now, repeating Hume's argument and assuming that there is no limit reached in the incremental extension of this range of values, we come to the conclusion that the range must be all the values from 0 to 1, and therefore we have no right to assign any one value rather than another.[5] But this argument is no better than the first version I have considered. Even if we assign ranges of values instead of definite values, these assignments will be made on the basis of a body of relevant evidence, and higher-order reflections about our ability to make such assignments will not seep down to affect these assignments themselves. Thus Hume's argument – even if we waive the problem of a limit – does not have its intended effect: higher order probability assignments concerning the correctness of our calculations do not seep down to affect either the specific probability or the range of probabilities of the statements they are about.[6]

I have spent time criticizing Hume's argument for two reasons: first, and rather incidentally, it is hard to let such an argument pass unchallenged. My second reason, which is more important for our present purposes, is to lay bare the fundamental principle of his argument. What, we can ask, is left of Hume's argument if we reject his claim that all probabilities must reduce "to nothing"? The answer, I think, is that the argument becomes a version of one of the traditional skeptical tropes: reason demands that every judgment be backed by a further judgment showing that the prior one is correct. This, after all, is the demand made in the prescriptive principle cited earlier:

> In every judgment, which we can form concerning probability, as well as concerning knowledge, we ought always to correct the first judgment, deriv'd from the nature of the object, by another judgment, deriv'd from the nature of the understanding. (pp. 181–2)

This leads, of course, to an infinite regress. Although Hume may have thought otherwise, this is the whole content of his argument. We might speculate that Hume was embarrassed to use this traditional argument with its sophistical appearance. Yet his argument turns upon it and, as we shall see, it is precisely the infinite regress that is the target of his naturalistic solution.[7]

Let us now look at Hume's naturalistic solution – his skeptical solution – to the unmitigated epistemological skepticism he accepts. After reviewing his argument, Hume asks himself the following question: *"how it happens, that even after all we retain a degree of belief, which is sufficient for our purpose, either in philosophy or common life."* He responds:

> I answer, that after the first and second decision; as the action of the mind becomes forc'd and unnatural, and the ideas faint and obscure; tho' the principles of judgment, and the balancing of opposite causes be the same as at the very beginning; yet their influence on the imagination, and the vigour they add to, or diminish from the thought, is by no means equal. . . . The attention is on the stretch: The posture of the mind is uneasy; and the spirits being diverted from their natural course, are not govern'd in their movements by the same laws, at least not to the same degree, as when they flow in their usual channel. (p. 185)

And then later on he says:

> 'Tis happy, therefore, that nature breaks the force of all sceptical arguments in time, and keeps them from having any considerable influence on the understanding. (p. 187)

Here Hume's exact phrasing is important: he argues that skeptical arguments do not have any *considerable* influence, for, if Hume is correct, the first few steps in our critical reflections do reduce the probability of an original judgment to some degree. But at a certain point the mind simply stops this process of higher order assessment even though the conceptual situation is unchanged. Being on the stretch it is no longer governed in its movements by the same laws. Thus it is the infinite regress of higher order assessments that is stopped – and only indirectly diminutions of probabilities – for the force of the beliefs becomes different and the natural laws of reason no longer apply.

Hume returns to this argument, giving it prominence, at the close of Book I:

Hume's Skepticism Concerning Reason

> I have already shewn, that the understanding, when it acts alone, and according to its most general principles, entirely subverts itself, and leaves not the lowest degree of evidence in any proposition, either in philosophy or common life. We save ourselves from this total scepticism only by means of that singular and seemingly trivial property of the fancy, by which we enter with difficulty into remote views of things, and are not able to accompany them with so sensible an impression, as we do those, which are more easy and natural. (pp. 267–8)

Hume is thus uncompromising in saying that understanding – when it acts alone – is thoroughly self-destructive. Understanding is not *self*-correcting.[8] The central idea is that a satisfactory equilibrium is achieved through the *balancing* of causal factors. The demands of understanding are important, for without them there would be no way to distinguish between a reasonable belief and sheer superstition. Yet a belief must always be a vector of these demands in conjunction with other causal influences. I take it to be one of the central concerns of the *Treatise* to forward this view of the operations of the human mind.

So far I have stressed – as Hume himself has stressed – the causal character of his theory. Yet the entire discussion presupposes another feature of Hume's naturalistic standpoint: his theory of belief. Hume asserts the connection between his concern with skeptical arguments and his theory of belief explicitly:

> My intention then in displaying so carefully the arguments of that fantastic sect, is only to make the reader sensible of the truth of my hypothesis, *that all our reasonings concerning causes and effects are deriv'd from nothing but custom: and that belief is more properly an act of the sensitive, than of the cogitative part of our natures*. I have here prov'd, that the very same principles, which make us form a decision upon any subject, and correct that decision by the consideration of our genius and capacity, and of the situation of our mind, when we examin'd that subject; I say, I have prov'd, that these same principles, when carry'd farther, and apply'd to every new reflex judgment, must, by continually diminishing the original evidence, at last reduce it to nothing, and utterly subvert all belief and opinion. If belief, therefore, were a simple act of the thought, without any peculiar manner of

conception, or the addition of a force and vivacity, it must infallibly destroy itself, and in every case terminate in a total suspense of judgment. (pp. 183–4)

The argument here is curious. Hume seems to think that only on his theory of belief can we explain why thought is not self-destructive. A theory that treats belief as a "simple act of thought," he suggests, cannot do this. But why? Suppose that I make a judgment in the normal way. I could then go on to perform higher order judgments as long as I wanted to and *also stop when I pleased*. Hume seems to think that any such acts of thought would have to be governed by the prescriptive rule that we must always form a higher order assessment of any judgment we make. At a certain point a person might simply abandon that rule – and that would be another simple act of thought. Here we would end our inquiries for no rational reason, but Hume's own position has that quality as well – indeed, he celebrates it.

Anyway, even if Hume's argument does not show what it is supposed to show, his intentions are plain. He holds that there is no rational response to the skeptical argument he has produced. He accepts a theoretical skepticism that is wholly unmitigated. He further holds that *only* on his theory of belief can we explain (though not justify) the occurrence of any belief whatsoever.[9]

It is now easy to see why, in the area of *epistemology*, Hume's prescriptive skepticism is narrowly circumscribed. A prescriptive skeptic recommends the suspension of belief (for some reason or other). For Hume, a belief is not a simple act of the thought; it is not something that we can choose to have; it is the result of certain causes. It is thus idle to recommend the suspension of belief when it is not in a person's power to do so.

> Nature, by an absolute and uncontroulable necessity has determin'd us to judge as well as to breath and feel; nor can we any more forbear viewing certain objects in a stronger and fuller light [i.e., believing them], upon account of their customary connexion with a present impression, than we can hinder ourselves from thinking as long as we are awake, or seeing the surrounding bodies, when we turn our eyes towards them in broad sunshine. (p. 183)

But Hume's position is, in fact, more subtle than it may first appear. He is not suggesting that skeptical arguments have *no* effect upon our beliefs. Unchecked by other causes, these arguments can have a dramatic impact:

> But what have I here said, that reflections very refin'd and metaphysical have little or no influence upon us? This opinion I can scarce forbear retracting, and condemning from my present feeling and experience. The *intense* view of these manifold contradictions and imperfections in human reason has so wrought upon me, and heated my brain, that I am ready to reject all belief and reasoning, and can look upon no opinion even as more probable or likely than another.
> (pp. 268–9)

Yet the intensity of these views disappears when one enters back into the "common affairs of life." Here we can chart our progress to moderate skepticism. We start out with our heads filled with beliefs – some drawn from common life, others from superstition and refined metaphysical speculation. We give the speculative side of our natures full play and are led into total skepticism. We then enter back into the affairs of common life and find that certain beliefs are inexorably forced back upon us. But not every opinion is restored, for some beliefs had no proper foundation in experience. In this way, skeptical reflections emancipate us from unnatural beliefs. The point is made in the *Enquiry*:

> The *imagination* of man is naturally sublime, delighted with whatever is remote and extraordinary, and running, without control, into the most distant parts of space and time in order to avoid the objects, which custom has rendered too familiar to it. A correct *Judgment* observes a contrary method, and avoiding all distant and high enquiries, confines itself to common life, and to such subjects as fall under daily practice and experience; leaving the more sublime topics to the embellishment of poets and orators, or to the arts of priests and politicians. *To bring us to so salutary a determination, nothing can be more serviceable, than to be once thoroughly convinced of the force of the Pyrrhonian doubt*, and of the impossibility, that anything, but the strong power of natural instinct, could free us from it. (*E.* p. 162, emphasis added)

This passage brings out exactly the extent of Hume's prescriptive

Hume's Skepticism Concerning Reason

skepticism. The same point can be brought out in a different way by comparing two prescriptive rules. The first, which has already been cited, appears at the beginning of Hume's discussion and serves an important dialectical purpose:

> In every judgment, which we can form concerning probability, as well as concerning knowledge, we ought always to correct the first judgment, deriv'd from the nature of the object, by another judgment, deriv'd from the nature of the understanding. (pp. 181–2)

Hume cannot accept this principle for, as he sees it, its unlimited application will lead to the total annihilation of all knowledge and probability. Near the close of this discussion he accepts a more modest canon that will give reason its place, but under a constraint that curbs its suicidal tendencies:

> Where reason is lively, and mixes itself with some propensity, it ought to be assented to. Where it does not, it never can have any title to operate upon us. (p. 270)

III

HUME'S ANSWER TO BAYLE'S SKEPTICISM CONCERNING EXTENSION

The second Part of Book I of the *Treatise* examines our ideas of space and time. It should be acknowledged from the start that this discussion does not show Hume at his best. At key points the argument turns upon embarrassing misunderstandings concerning infinity, and the view that he comes to at the end has found no champions. Even so, there are few portions of the text that reveal Hume's general strategy in a clearer way. His task, of course, is to give an adequate account of the nature and origin of our ideas of space and time. Standing squarely in the path of this enterprise is a skeptical argument formulated by Bayle intended to show that these concepts are unintelligible. It is Bayle's *conceptual* skepticism concerning extension that sets Hume his problem, and his constructive account of these notions is formulated explicitly as an answer to his skepticism.[1]

Let me sketch briefly Bayle's arguments and then examine the conclusions (or, rather, the morals) he draws from them. Bayle suggests that a person who wishes to revive Zeno's paradoxes showing the impossibility of motion could begin by showing that extension itself is a paradoxical idea.

> There is no extension; therefore there is no motion. The inference is valid; for what has no extension occupies no space; and what occupies no space cannot go from one place to another, nor consequently move.... The only difficulty then is to prove that there is no extension. Here is what Zeno could put forth. Extension cannot be made up of either

mathematical points, atoms, or particles that are divisible to infinity; therefore its existence is impossible.[2]

Extension cannot be made up of mathematical points, since it is obvious "that several nonentities of extension joined together will never make up an extension."[3] It cannot be made up of material points or atoms:

> for every extension, no matter how small it may be, has a right and a left side. . . . Therefore, it is a collection of distinct bodies. I can deny concerning the right side what I affirm about the left side. These two sides are not in the same place. A body cannot be in two places both at the same time, and consequently every extension that occupies several parts of space contains several bodies.[4]

The attack upon infinite divisibility is longer and more diffuse. The fundamental objection is first stated in these words:

> An infinite number of parts of extension, each of which is extended and distinct from all the others, both with regard to its being and to the place that it occupies, cannot be contained in a space one hundred million times smaller than the hundred thousandth part of a grain of barley.[5]

Less whimsically, Bayle is arguing (of course, incorrectly) that a body composed of infinitely many finite parts must be *infinite* in extension. This comes out explicitly when he argues that two distinct objects could not occupy the same plane, "for each requires an infinite space, since it contains an infinity of extended bodies."[6]

Given Bayle's own prefatory remarks, we might expect him to conclude that extension does not exist. In fact, he does not draw this conclusion but argues instead that extension cannot exist "outside our minds."[7] He repeats this claim when he speaks of the "use of geometrical demonstrations against the existence of extension." "They serve no other use," he says, "but show that extension exists only in our understanding."[8] There are intimations of Kant in this passage, but Kant gave the doctrine of the ideality of space and time an important development by treating them as *forms* of experience rather than *contents* within experience. Bayle's position shows no such sophistication. He seems to

Hume's Answer to Bayle's Skepticism

suggest that a concept that admits of no consistent interpretation cannot, for that reason, be realized outside of the mind, but can, in some way, still be realized within the understanding. This is a strange idea and, as we shall see in a moment, Hume will have none of it.

Hume's own reasoning concerning space and time passes through the following stages:

1. Whatever we might say about space and time themselves, our ideas of space and time are not infinitely divisible but ultimately resolve themselves into parts that are "perfectly simple and indivisible."
2. What is true of an idea must be at least *possible* for the object of that idea.
3. Where something is possible, there can be no *a priori* argument showing that it is not the case.
4. Hence there can be no *a priori* argument showing that space and time are not composed of parts that are perfectly simple and indivisible and so, of course, there is no *a priori* proof that space and time are infinitely divisible.
5. According to Bayle, space and time must be composed of infinitely divisible parts, pure mathematical points, or physical atoms. Since all three alternatives lead to impossible results, a further possibility must be found.
6. The alternative and correct possibility is that space is composed of extensionless points endowed with colour or solidity.

Without spending too much time on the obvious flaws in this argument it is worth following it out in detail, for again this will show us important features of Hume's methods and intentions.

(1) Hume offers two arguments intended to show that our ideas of space and time are not infinitely divisible. The first blends a platitude with a conceptual confusion. The platitude is that the human mind is not capable of performing an infinite division of some magnitude. The conceptual confusion, which will infect all of Hume's discussion of infinite divisibility, is given in these words: " 'Tis also obvious, that whatever is capable of being divided *in infinitum*, must consist of an infinite number of parts" (p. 26). This claim turns upon a faulty analogy with the finite division of a magnitude into parts. If we insist upon talking about the *parts*

that result from an infinite division, we must realize that the concept of a part is then used in a different sense than when we speak about the parts that emerge from finitely many divisions. This is the modern response to Bayle's skeptical argument, for, worked out in detail, it provides the alternative needed to block it. Here it is sufficient to notice what is wrong with the Bayle-Hume treatment of infinite divisibility; there is no need to pursue the matter in detail.[9]

Hume's second argument for (1) turns upon the claim that *in fact* experience reveals minimal perceptibilia – both in imagination and perception. Here *minimal* means incapable of further division. Perhaps it is best to point out what Hume is *not* arguing. He is not suggesting that there are things so minute that we are incapable of imagining them. He calls this an "error of common opinion" and goes on to say, rather quaintly: "that we can form ideas, which shall be no greater than the smallest atom of the animal spirits of an insect a thousand times less than a mite" (p. 28). Despite the exact wording, I think that Hume here must mean that we can form an idea *of* such a thing, but I confess that I am not sure of this. In any case, it is clear that Hume is not saying that there is some minimal *extension* limiting the imagination. The above passage continues as follows:

> And we ought rather to conclude, that the difficulty lies in enlarging our conceptions so much as to form a just notion of a mite, or even of an insect a thousand times less than a mite. For in order to form a just notion of these animals, we must have a distinct idea representing every part of them. (p. 28)

Thus to imagine the ten thousandth part of a mite (or anything) I must have a distinct conception of something with ten thousand parts, but this distinct conception, Hume argues, is quite beyond the power of the imagination. Thus every image must contain constituents that are minimal in the sense of not being capable of further division. This is precisely the thesis he maintains:

> 'Tis therefore certain, that the imagination reaches a *minimum*, and may raise up to itself an idea, of which it cannot conceive any sub-division, and which cannot be diminished without a total annihilation. (p. 27)

Hume's Answer to Bayle's Skepticism

Hume makes the same claim about impressions of sense:

> Put a spot of ink upon paper, fix your eye upon that spot, and retire to such a distance, that at last you lose sight of it; 'tis plain, that the moment before it vanish'd the image or impression was perfectly indivisible. (p. 27)

Again, Hume is not arguing that we cannot see things that fall below a minimum size, for this can be altered by using a microscope or telescope. "Both," he says, "give parts to impressions, which to the naked eye appear simple and uncompounded, and advances to a *minimum*, what was formerly imperceptible" (p. 28). So what will count as minimal will depend upon the context of perception, but all perception is composed of minimal (indivisible) perceptions. In any given context, a perception will count as minimal if its further division will produce its utter annihilation.

Few modern writers will have much patience with this line of argument. For what vanished or seemed to vanish was the spot and the spot was divisible both before and after it vanished or seemed to vanish. Hume, however, speaks of the impression or image itself vanishing and being indivisible just before it vanished. It is very difficult to find your footing in this argument. We might make sense out of this claim that the impression vanished by translating it into: the spot seemed to vanish. But this produces no candidate for indivisibility. We can also make sense out of the claim that the impression is indivisible by translating it into: just before the spot seems to vanish it seems to be indivisible. This, however, is just false. What is true is this: given the situation just before the spot seems to vanish, if we had cut the spot in half and separated the two parts, we could not have seen either of them. From this perspective Hume's argument seems to involve the following fallacious inference:

> We are aware of something which, if divided and separated, *we could not be aware of at all*.
> We are aware of an indivisible something.

But enough of this; Hume believes that he has found an item in experience that is indivisible. We can now see how he exploits this conclusion.

(2) Here is Hume's statement of the second step of the argument I have outlined above:

Hume's Answer to Bayle's Skepticism

> 'Tis an establish'd maxim in metaphysics, *That whatever the mind clearly conceives includes the idea of possible existence,* or in other words, *that nothing we imagine is absolutely impossible.* (p. 32)

In applying this principle, Hume seems to take it for granted that we will never misdescribe what we clearly conceive or imagine. For clear cases at least, we will never think that we have imagined one thing when, in fact, we have imagined something else. I do not see why this is true and Hume himself has no steady opinion about our fallibility and infallibility in understanding our own ideas. Later in this same discussion Hume argues that people are mistaken in their belief that they have an idea of a vacuum:

> The frequent disputes concerning a vacuum, or extension without matter, prove not the reality of the idea, upon which the dispute turns; there being nothing more common, than to see men deceive themselves in this particular. (p. 62)

That is, nothing is more common than to see men deceive themselves concerning the reality of an idea. On the other side, Hume constantly appeals to imaginability with no qualms about the possibility that we may have misunderstood the nature of the thing imagined (see the next passage cited in the text). A skeptical doubt at this point would, of course, overthrow one of his favorite patterns of argument.[10]

(3) and (4) The third and fourth steps of Hume's argument, as I have sketched it, are given in this paragraph:

> Now 'tis certain we have an idea of extension; for otherwise why do we talk and reason concerning it? 'Tis likewise certain, that this idea, as conceiv'd by the imagination, tho' divisible into parts or inferior ideas, is not infinitely divisible, nor consists of an infinite number of parts: For that exceeds the comprehension of our limited capacities. Here then is an idea of extension, which consists of parts or inferior ideas, that are perfectly indivisible: consequently this idea implies no contradiction: consequently 'tis possible for extension really to exist conformable to it: and consequently all the arguments employ'd against the possibility of mathematical points are mere scholastick quibbles, and unworthy of our attention. (p. 32)

Hume's Answer to Bayle's Skepticism

Here Hume speaks as a defender of the doctrine of *mathematical points*, though this does not accurately (or fully) characterize his own final position.[11]

(5) It becomes clear as the argument unfolds that Hume has an eye toward Bayle's threefold classification of possible theories of extension: that the parts of space must be either infinitely divisible, extensionless, or, to use Bayle's word, atoms, i.e., physical points. In the following passage, Hume mentions these three possibilities, adding a fourth which, he suggests, provides a correct solution.

> It has often been maintain'd in the schools, that extension must be divisible, *in infinitum*, because the system of mathematical points is absurd; and that system is absurd, because a mathematical point is a non-entity, and consequently can never by its conjunction with others form a real existence. This wou'd be perfectly decisive, were there no medium betwixt the infinite divisibility of matter, and the non-entity of mathematical points. But there is evidently a medium, *viz.* the bestowing a colour or solidity on these points; and the absurdity of both extremes is a demonstration of the truth and reality of this medium. The system of *physical points*, which is another medium, is too absurd to need a refutation. (p. 40)

Hume nowhere considers further alternatives.

From the above passage we already know what is wrong with the doctrine of mathematical points: a conjunction of non-entities can never form a real extension. The system of physical points is, he claims, "too absurd to need refutation." What is wrong with the doctrine of infinite divisibility? Hume has a number of arguments on this topic – all bad – but they finally come down to a single argument or at least to the confusion that underlies it:

> Upon the whole, I conclude, that the idea of an infinite number of parts is individually the same idea with that of an infinite extension; that no finite extension is capable of containing an infinite number of parts; and consequently that no finite extension is infinitely divisible. (p. 30)

Over against Hume's arguments are certain geometric demonstrations that are intended to prove *a priori* that a finite extension is infinitely divisible. Hume does not attack these proofs in detail.

Instead he argues that the mathematician's standard of equality in geometry is not exact and therefore cannot form the basis of demonstrative argument. It is not exact, Hume argues, because equality or congruency can be perfectly established only by showing that two lines or two areas are composed of the very same number of points, and that is something we are never able to do. This causes no practical problems, since we can make the comparisons fine enough for our purposes. It does show, however, that geometry falls short of the demonstrative standards of arithmetic and algebra. Thus there are no geometric demonstrations of infinite divisibility just because there are no geometric demonstrations at all.[12]

(6) What, then, is this medium that Hume finds between extensionless points and infinite divisibility? He suggests extensionless sensibilia: extensionless color points or extensionless tangible points. Returning to Bayle's criticism, would such a point have both a right side and a left side? I suppose that the answer to this must be yes, for something could be on the right side of such a point and something else could be on the left side of that point. For example, the right side of the point might be contiguous with something green, the left side contiguous with something red. From this Bayle would argue that the point must now divide into parts, for something is true of one feature that is not true of the other. Since the point now has parts, it can be divided. Hume's ingenious reply is that no such division is possible, for, if attempted, it would not yield two things but, instead, the annihilation of the one thing. In a manner of speaking, Hume's minimal sensibilia are intermediate between mathematical points (which are not enough) and physical points (which are too much).

Forgetting all the false moves that occur in this argument, we can notice the part it plays in Hume's discussion. The introduction of these simple and indivisible perceptual points does *not* give Hume's theory of the origin of our ideas of space and time. Our idea of space, for example, is not derived from the sum of such points, but rather, from the *manner* in which they are disposed to one another. We can look at that theory in a moment. The task of the argument so far is to respond to Bayle's claim that upon *every* possible interpretation extension emerges as unintelligible. Answering this argument is a necessary antecedent to the

Hume's Answer to Bayle's Skepticism

constructive task of explaining the origins of our ideas of space and time which we shall now examine.

At the beginning of Section IV, Hume says that his "system concerning space and time consists of two parts, which are intimately connected together" (p. 39). The first, he says, establishes that "no idea of extension or duration consists of an infinite number of parts or inferior ideas, but of a finite number, and these simple and indivisible" (p. 39). The second part of his argument is intended to distinguish his position from the view that mathematical points are sheer nonentities:

> these indivisible parts, being nothing in themselves, are
> inconceivable when not fill'd with something real and
> existent. The ideas of space and time are therefore no separate
> or distinct ideas, but merely those of the manner or order,
> in which objects exist. (pp. 39–40)

Here an important shift takes place. Earlier it seemed natural to assume that Hume had introduced a theory of minimal perceptions as parts of the whole that make up an extension. Indeed, certain passages cannot be read in any other way. Without this claim, Hume's response to Bayle is not correct even in form. Yet in the passage just cited, Hume says that these indivisible parts are "nothing in themselves." The indivisible parts are quite extensionless yet still in some manner are filled with something real and existent. It is hard to understand the metaphor of something extensionless being "filled,"[13] but, more importantly, Hume, on this interpretation, moves toward a relational rather than an atomistic theory of space and time. Much of Hume's prose points in this direction. Here is what he says about space:

> But my senses convey to me only the impressions of colour'd
> points, dispos'd in a certain manner. If the eye is sensible of
> anything farther, I desire it may be pointed out to me. But if
> it be impossible to shew any thing farther, we may conclude
> with certainty, that the idea of extension is nothing but a copy
> of these colour'd points, and of the manner of their
> appearance. (p. 34)

This suggests that spatial relations emerge out of relationships *between* the basic color points and are not summed up from the basic extensionality within each color point. The suggestion comes out more clearly when Hume speaks about time:

> The idea of time is not deriv'd from a particular impression mix'd up with others, and plainly distinguishable from them; but arises altogether from the manner, in which impressions appear to the mind, without making one of the number. Five notes play'd on a flute give us the impression and idea of time; tho' time be not a sixth impression, which presents itself to the hearing or any other of the senses. (p. 36)

Hume adds that it cannot be a sixth impression "which the mind by reflection finds in itself," for impressions of reflection involve the excitation of emotion (p. 36).

As an aside, in this passage Hume seems to abandon his basic principle that every idea must be derived from some act of corresponding impressions. Yet it is not clear to me that this criticism is just. What Hume says is that an impression of time (from which the idea of time is derived) is not a *sixth* impression, and by that he seems to mean not a sixth impression of a kind with the five impressions of the notes. In order to stay with his official theory, he must mean that the impression of time is an entirely different order: we have an impression of the manner in which other impressions appear. It may be natural to think that impressions must always be of individuals but, as far as I can see, nothing in Hume's position requires this.[14]

But to return to the main point: this passage about our ideas of time again suggests a relational theory rather than a part-whole theory. Yet Hume continually speaks of these extensionless minima as parts of space. There is, however, a good reason why Hume must reject the idea that these minimal color points are parts of space: since they are extensionless – rather than minimal finite extensions – they will not sum up to a finite whole. This, of course, was Bayle's argument against the claim that extension is made up out of mathematical points. What seems to happen is this: Hume begins with a minimum part theory suggested to him by the phenomenon of minimal perceptibilia. He uses this theory in his response to Bayle both to block the process of endless division and to reject the demonstrative character of geometrical proofs of infinite divisibility. When he turns to his positive account, he realizes that his extensionless color points – though

Hume's Answer to Bayle's Skepticism

more than nothing – are not more than nothing in a way that makes them an improvement over mathematical points as parts of space. This insight led Hume to sketch, however crudely, a relational theory of space and time. I do not think that Hume recognized that the theory he developed to answer Bayle is not the same as the theory he developed to give a positive account of the origin of our ideas of space and time. Nor did he see that these two theories have opposite tendencies. He believed just the opposite. He thought that he had produced a theory that gave the correct conceptual account of our ideas of space and time (clearing them of skeptical attacks) and further gave the correct explanation of how these ideas arise out of impressions.

After relying heavily upon Norman Kemp Smith's discussion of space and time, it may seem ungracious to end on a dissenting note. Risking this, I shall point out an important respect in which our approaches differ. Kemp Smith claims that Hume treats Bayle's "method of argument as a direct challenge to the defense of reason."

> What I would wish to emphasize is that his main motive in denying space and time to be infinitely divisible, and in his consequent heterodox treatment of geometry, was his desire to vindicate for reason the right to have jurisdiction in every field of possible human knowledge, with no limitation save such as is prescribed by the absence or insufficiency of the data required for dealing with them.[15]

This passage suggests that Hume is prepared to defend reason's claim over a broad territory, but in what follows, this suggestion is taken back. Kemp Smith is here speaking of reason in a *strict* sense, where it is limited to *demonstrative* (and, I suppose, intuitive) knowledge.[16] Indeed, he criticizes Hume for not always being careful to distinguish between reason "properly so called" from reason in a "popular sense" where it is a "faculty supposed to be capable of determining moral distinctions and of justifying beliefs in regard to matters of fact and existence."[17] Concerning reason in this popular sense, he tells us:

> This so-called "reason," Hume maintains, is merely a misnomer for instinctively determined sentiments and beliefs. Accordingly he was not departing from or qualifying his

defence of reason, he was further substantiating it, in proceeding to show that this so-called reason has no right to the title.[18]

I find all this both peculiar and counter-textual. It is a central feature of Hume's program to deny anything beyond an ancillary role to reason in all matters of value, fact, and existence. Reason's claims are limited to the demonstrative truths of mathematics and, perhaps, logic. Furthermore, in the present discussion, geometry, one of the central achievements of mathematics and the historical paradigm of a rationally developed discipline, is removed from its domain. Finally, Hume is not even willing to defend the claims of reason in this narrow domain. As we have seen, the skepticism with regard to reason shows that the principles of reason, left to themselves, destroy even the warrant for demonstrative truths. Not only in its "popular" sense, but reason "properly so-called" is also grounded in "instinctively determined sentiments and beliefs."

If Kemp Smith's position is more carefully and modestly stated, it does, in fact, have a point. Although no text in the *Treatise* shows this explicitly, Hume may have had an important additional motive for attacking the doctrine of infinite divisibility: it had been exploited by the Port Royal Jansenists for purposes he would abhor. Presumably Hume was acquainted with *L'Art de Penser*, the so-called *Port-Royal Logic*, but he would have found the following passage from that work cited by Bayle in the discussion of Zeno of Elea:

> The value that can be gained from these speculations
> [concerning infinite divisibility] is not simply that of acquiring
> this sort of knowledge, which is pretty sterile in itself; but it
> is in learning to know the limits of our mind and in making
> it admit, in spite of itself, that there are things that exist though
> it is not capable of understanding them. For this reason it is
> good that we wear it out with these subtleties in order to check
> its presumption and to keep it from ever being foolhardy
> enough to oppose its feeble light to the truths that the Church
> proposes to it on the pretext that it cannot understand them.[19]

Although Hume concludes, at the furthest extreme of his reflections, that there is no rational foundation for *any* of our commitments, he would have no patience with commitments to the irrational, i.e., to ideas with no coherent or intelligible content. If this is what is meant by describing Hume as a defender of reason, then so be it, but this in no way mitigates the total epistemological skepticism that lies at the heart of his system.

IV

CAUSALITY, NECESSITY, AND INDUCTION

No portion of the *Treatise* has received more attention than the discussion of the interrelated notions of causality, necessity, and induction. For this reason it is difficult to say anything that has not been said before. All the same, I think that Hume's treatment of these topics is much more complex than generally assumed, and, although this may seem presumptuous, I do not think that any interpreter has seen how the various major themes fit together to form a coherent whole. There are a number of reasons for this. First, many of Hume's arguments, for example, his skeptical attack upon induction and his attempted regularity definition of causation, have intrinsic philosophical interest that tempts the commentator to excise them from their textual setting and then explicate and evaluate them on their own terms. That Hume's arguments tolerate such displacement shows that they possess merit beyond the particular philosophical framework in which they were developed. The danger, of course, is that Hume's own thought and writing may come to have, at best, only an *ancestral* relationship to what comes to be known as the *Humean* position on some topic. Second, it is natural, and not altogether wrong, to take the discussion in Sections 4 through 7 of the *Enquiry* as a guide to the fundamental structure of Part III, Book I of the *Treatise*. But something new is added in the *Enquiry*: there the skeptical argument concerning induction is developed within the framework of an *explicitly* stated distinction between Relations of Ideas and Matters of Fact.[1] There are also a number of themes missing, or at least strongly muted, in the *Enquiry*. One is a

Causality, Necessity, and Induction

complex dialectical development that allows Hume to use his skeptical argument concerning induction to remove an obstacle to his analysis of necessity and causation. This is the central theme of the present chapter. Hume's skepticism concerning induction has a second important role in the *Treatise*: it prepares the way for the triumph of the imagination as the primary faculty for the fixation of belief. I discuss this in the next chapter.

How does Hume describe our ideas of causality and necessity and how, in the end, does he relate them? One answer is that causality is a particular kind of necessity or, at the very least, necessity is an essential constituent of causality. Norman Kemp Smith, correcting what he takes to be the mistakes of others, attributes such a view to Hume:

> Hume is no supporter of what is usually meant by the "uniformity" view of causation. As he is careful to insist, causation is more than sequence, and more also than invariable sequence. We distinguish between mere sequence and causal sequence; and what differentiates the two is that the idea of necessitation (determination or agency) enters into the latter as a quite essential element.[2]

To back this claim, he cites the following passage from the *Treatise*:

> Shall we then rest contented with these two relations of contiguity and succession, as affording a compleat idea of causation? By no means. An object may be contiguous and prior to another, without being consider'd as its cause. There is a *NECESSARY CONNEXION* to be taken into consideration; and that relation is of much greater importance, than any of the other two above-mention'd. (p. 77)

The clear suggestion of this passage is that a reference to necessity must occur in any correct definition of causation. But if we examine the text further to verify this claim, we get mixed results. Hume's first definition reads as follows:

> We may define a CAUSE to be 'An object precedent and contiguous to another, and where all the objects resembling the former are plac'd in like relations of precedency and contiguity to those objects, that resemble the latter.' (p. 170)

Causality, Necessity, and Induction

This definition contains no reference to necessitation, or at least none that is transparent. Hume's second definition does seem to contain such a reference:

> A CAUSE is an object precedent and contiguous to another, and so united with it, that the idea of the one determines the mind to form the idea of the other, and the impression of the one to form a more lively idea of the other. (p. 170)

Here Hume speaks of *determination*, which seems to be a causal notion, thus inviting the charge of circularity, but he does not speak of *necessitation*, and it is not clear that Kemp Smith has a right to use them interchangeably. There is, however, at least one passage that gives unambiguous support to Kemp Smith's side of the argument. It occurs in Book II: "According to my definitions, necessity makes an essential part of causation" (p. 407).

This passage may seem to settle the issue in Kemp Smith's favor, but just a few pages later, Hume makes another remark that deeply obscures his position:

> I define necessity two ways, conformable to the two definitions of *cause*, of which it makes an essential part. I place it either in the constant union and conjunction of like objects, or in the inference of the mind from the one to the other. (p. 409)

Here, in consecutive sentences, Hume repeats his claim that necessity is an essential part of a cause and then offers a uniformity interpretation of necessity itself. His discussion has thus moved through the following stages: he begins by giving two definitions of cause, the first of a uniformity or regularity kind. Kemp Smith suggests, with support from the text, that this regularity definition must be supplemented with a reference to necessity, but when we look at Hume's account of necessity, we find the pattern repeated: two definitions are offered, the first again of a regularity kind. The suggestion that this new regularity definition must itself be supplemented by a further reference to necessity leads, of course, to a bad infinite regress.

I confess that I do not know how to bring these passages into alignment. All the same, I think it is possible to extract from the text of the *Treatise* Hume's most carefully considered views concerning causality, necessity, and the relationships between them. Furthermore, if we observe the manner in which Hume's

Causality, Necessity, and Induction

position actually unfolds in the text – in particular, the way in which the argument undergoes a profound reversal under the influence of Hume's skepticism concerning induction – I think we can make some sense out of Hume's tendency to produce passages that point in opposite directions. Since for my purposes it is important to preserve a simple narrative line, I have placed most of the critical and scholarly remarks in the footnotes and in two appendices at the end of the book.

For Hume, causality is a kind of relation, so he begins by explaining how this relation fits into the system of other relations. He first divides relations into two classes: "such as depend entirely on the ideas, which we compare together, and such as may be chang'd without any change in the ideas" (p. 69). Although it is not obvious that he is right in doing so, Hume places causal relations in the second category.[3] However, for our purposes, Hume's next move is more significant. He makes a further division within the second class of relations:

> it appears, that of those three relations, which depend not upon the mere ideas, the only one, that can be trac'd beyond our senses, and informs us of existences and objects, which we do not see or feel, is *causation*. (p. 74)

It is just this feature of causation, that it provides a basis for belief beyond the perceived or remembered, that gives it paramount importance in Hume's system. Initially, we can state Hume's question in the following way: how do causal relations provide the basis (the ground, support, or warrant) for an inference from the perceived to the unperceived? At the start, at least, it seems appropriate to demand that any adequate definition of causal relations provide an answer to this question.

Hume begins his investigation by considering a single instance of a causal relation. Under inspection, he claims to find only two features connecting the causal relata that are relevant to the causal relation that obtains between them: contiguity and priority. The cause and effect must be spatially and temporally contiguous, and the cause must be prior to its effect. But he considers these relations, though necessary,[4] "imperfect and unsatisfactory," for as he states, without citing an instance, "an object may be contiguous and prior to another, without being consider'd as its cause" (p. 77). Furthermore, Hume identifies the deficiency of any such definition: "There is a NECESSARY CONNEXION to be taken into consideration; and that relation is of much greater importance, than any of the other two above-mention'd" (p. 77). This, of course, is the passage Kemp Smith relies upon to show that Hume was not a "supporter of what is usually meant by the 'uniformity' view of causation." I shall argue that Kemp Smith totally misunderstands the role of this passage in the development of Hume's argument.

Why should the relation of a necessary connection be of more importance than the relations of contiguity and priority? The answer is obvious if we keep in mind that Hume's main concern at this stage of his discussion is to understand the basis of an *inference* from the perceived to the unperceived. For Hume, spatio-temporal relations cannot serve this purpose, because they are given *within* experience as the manner in which indivisible perceptibles are disposed to one another. The thought that space and time apply to unperceived objects itself stands in need of explanation, and that explanation, as we shall see, is itself causal.[5] A necessary connection is obviously a better candidate for grounding this inference, for given a perception of an object and the perception of a necessary connection, perhaps we will have the basis for the transition for the perceived object to an unperceived object. Hume's present difficulty is that he cannot find in experience any such necessary connection relating even actual perceptions.

Since his quarry has eluded him, Hume suggests that we, like hunters, "beat about all the neighbouring fields" in the hope that good fortune will help us in our search (p. 78). He selects two neighboring fields for beating. First he raises this question: "For what reason [do] we pronounce it *necessary*, that every thing whose existence has a beginning, shou'd also have a cause?" (p. 78). The reasoning here anticipates one half of the dilemma that Hume will pose for inductive reasoning. In particular, he concludes that since the maxim that *whatever begins to exist, must have a cause of existence* is not derived "from knowledge or any scientific reasoning," it must therefore "necessarily arise from observation and experience" (p. 82).

For our purposes, Hume starts a more interesting hare in the second neighboring field by asking:

Causality, Necessity, and Induction

> Why we conclude, that such particular causes must *necessarily* have such particular effects; and what is the nature of that *inference* we draw from the one to the other, and of the *belief* we repose in it. (p. 78)

Here necessity is still interlocked with the inference from cause to effect (and conversely) that interests him.

Since Hume was already stymied when examining a single case of a causal relation, he turns now to classes of cases. For reasons that will become evident later, he introduces his cardinal doctrine as a statement of psychological fact:

> We remember to have had frequent instances of the existence of one species of objects; and also remember, that the individuals of another species of objects have always attended them, and have existed in a regular order of contiguity and succession with regard to them. . . . Without any farther ceremony, we call the one *cause* and the other *effect*, and infer the existence of the one from that of the other. (p. 87)

We now have a new idea to add to the relations of contiguity and priority found in the previous examination of a single case: the *constant conjunction* of these objects in a class of similar cases. Hume's initial (and perhaps feigned) response to this discovery is disappointment:

> to tell the truth, this new-discover'd relation of a constant conjunction seems to advance us but little in our way . . . [for] from the mere repetition of any past impression, even to infinity, there will never arise any new original idea, such as that of a necessary connexion; and the number of impressions has in this case no more effect than if we confin'd ourselves to one only. (p. 88)

It is important to characterize Hume's worries with some care, for, as we shall see, he will follow out one line of reasoning and then reverse himself and adopt another. Hume notes, as a fact, that we make inferences from known to unknown instances after enjoying an extended experience of two sorts of things constantly conjoined. Yet this practice, however natural, seems lacking in rational foundation. In order to provide a rational foundation for this inference, some third idea must be found that will serve as a mediating link underwriting inferences from cause to effect and effect to cause. The obvious candidate for this mediating link is, of course, that of a necessary connection. Hume's initial worry, though not his ultimate worry, is that he cannot see how the repetition of a conjunction of ideas can give rise to "any new original idea, such as that of a necessary connexion." Thus Hume might have reached his famous skeptical conclusion concerning induction by reasoning in the following way: we need the idea of a necessary connection to justify projecting regularities found in experience beyond experience, but the experience of past regularities – no matter how extensive – is never capable of generating this new idea. Thus our inductive arguments are without foundation. But for Hume this is a road not taken, and if we reflect for a moment, we can see why it is not open to him. Hume shifted his attention to the assignment of particular causes and effects in the hope that examining this operation of the human understanding would shed light on the nature of necessity. Hume never questions the assumption that some idea must be associated with the words "necessary connexion." He is not, that is, a conceptual skeptic concerning them. Thus any argument that makes our idea of a necessary connection either impossible or inexplicable runs counter to the main development in the text.

So it seems that Hume is still stymied. The idea of a necessary connection is the natural candidate for explaining causal inferences from perceived to unperceived instances, but he is still unable to give an adequate account of the origin of this idea. This brings us to the decisive point in the text that changes Hume's whole way of viewing the problem of necessity. Instead of continuing his direct search for a connecting link between events that might sanction causal inferences, he raises a perfectly general question: what assumption are we making when we project past regularities into the future? His answer is that any such reasoning "wou'd proceed upon that principle, *that instances, of which we have had no experience, must resemble those, of which we have had experience, and that the course of nature continues always uniformly the same*" (p. 89). Having exposed this principle as the foundation of all causal reasoning, he asks for its justification, and then at a perfectly general level, he proceeds to "consider all the arguments, upon which such a proposition may be suppos'd to be founded" (p. 89). He cannot, of course, consider *all* arguments

Causality, Necessity, and Induction

that might support this principle, so instead he considers all the *forms* of argument that might be brought forth to support the principle of the uniformity of nature. These, he tells us, are only two in number, for they "must be deriv'd either from *knowledge* or *probability*" (p. 89). Since, as he will argue, neither form of argument can be used to justify the principle of the uniformity of nature, we arrive at what has come to be known as Hume's skepticism concerning induction.

Since the validity of Hume's skeptical argument is not our present concern, we can sketch its main features in a rough and ready way. Echoing the results of his excursion into the first neighboring field, Hume first argues "that there can be no *demonstrative* arguments to prove *that these instances, of which we have had no experience, resemble those, of which we have had experience*" for we can "at least conceive a change in the course of nature" and what is not "absolutely impossible" is immune to "any pretended demonstration against it" (p. 89). This suggests that the principle that nature is uniform must be based upon probabilistic considerations concerning observation and experience. But this, for Hume the only remaining alternative, will not do either, for

> probability is founded on the presumption of a resemblance betwixt those objects, of which we have had experience, and those, of which we have had none; and therefore 'tis impossible this presumption can arise from probability.
> (p. 90)

The corresponding passage in the *Enquiry* makes the same point with more clarity:

> We have said that all arguments concerning existence are founded on the relation of cause and effect; that our knowledge of that relation is derived entirely from experience; and that all our experimental conclusions proceed upon the supposition that the future will be conformable to the past. To endeavour, therefore, the proof of this last supposition by probable arguments, or arguments regarding existence, must be evidently going in a circle, and taking that for granted, which is the very point in question.
> (*E.*, pp. 35–6)

Causality, Necessity, and Induction

Since Hume concludes that no argument can justify our inductive inferences because no argument can justify the uniformity principle upon which they rely, I shall call this Hume's *no-argument argument*. I defend this interpretation of Hume's argument in detail in Appendix A, where I also examine various responses to it. In this chapter and the next, I shall concentrate on the role that this argument plays in the development of Hume's position.

What kind of skeptical argument is this? Interestingly, and probably contrary to Hume's own intentions, it is best classified as an instance of an *antecedent* skepticism rather than a *consequent* skepticism. The argument is *a priori* in form and does not rest upon scientific enquiry that reveals the fallaciousness of our mental faculties. Of course, the argument is theoretical as opposed to prescriptive in its intentions. Hume challenges the warrant for the principle that nature is uniform, and with this challenges all our inductive inferences which, as he thinks, depend upon it. He does not recommend that we suspend belief concerning this principle or abandon the inductive practices it underlies. Furthermore, within its domain of application, Hume has generated an epistemological skepticism that is wholly unmitigated. Every inductive argument, even those with only a probabilistic conclusion, relies upon the principle that nature is uniform, and since that suppressed premise (or rule of inference) is in principle unjustified, so too are all particular inductive inferences.

Of course, Hume is not a conceptual skeptic in this area. He nowhere suggests that our inductive inferences are unintelligible. Nor does he suggest this with respect to the notions of causality and necessary connection. In fact, and this is the central thesis of this chapter, Hume's skepticism concerning induction plays a crucial role in allowing him to complete his account of our idea of a necessary connection and thus avoid conceptual skepticism. We have been given a perfectly general argument to the effect that nothing can rationally underwrite our projection of past regularities into the future. Since this was the presumptive role assigned to our idea of a necessary connection (and the supposed feature of that idea that made it important), Hume is now in a position to consider this idea from quite a different perspective.

We may recall that Hume's initial worry about the idea of a necessary connection took the following form:

Causality, Necessity, and Induction

From the mere repetition of any past impression, even to infinity, there never will arise any new original idea, such as that of a necessary connexion; and the number of impressions has in this case no more effect than if we confin'd ourselves to one only. (p. 88)

But now that Hume has rejected the notion that any idea – including the idea of a necessary connection – can justify our projecting past regularities into the future, he is systematically free to reverse his field and argue and reason in the following way:

upon farther enquiry I find, that the repetition is not in every particular the same, but produces a new impression, and by that means the idea, which I at present examine. For after frequent repetition, I find, that upon the appearance of one of the objects, the mind is *determin'd* by custom to consider its usual attendant, and to consider it in a stronger light upon account of its relation to the first object. 'Tis this impression, then, or *determination*, which affords me the idea of necessity. (Hume's italics, pp. 155–6)

When I say that Hume is systematically free to reverse his field, I mean this: since Hume has abandoned the idea of grounding our causal inference in the idea of a necessary connection, there is nothing wrong now in giving an account of our idea of a necessary connection through the use of transparently causal notions. To use Hume's official language, our idea of a necessary connection is derived from an impression of *reflection*; in particular, by the mind's activity of making a transition from one idea to another in a customary and undeviating manner.

The idea of necessity arises from some impression. There is no impression convey'd by our senses, which can give rise to that idea. It must, therefore, be deriv'd from some internal impression, or impression of reflexion. There is no internal impression, which has any relation to the present business, but that propensity, which custom produces, to pass from an object to the idea of its usual attendant. This therefore is the essence of necessity. (p. 165)

This development has an important implication: where Hume

previously assumed that the idea of a necessary connection must form part of the definition of causal relations, he ends up by sharply separating these two notions. Of course, whenever we *believe* that a causal relation obtains between two objects, we will also *feel* a necessary connection between them. The two ideas are, therefore, naturally associated. Given this, an account of causal *inferring* should discuss both ideas. Nonetheless, the ideas are different and separate. We can show this by comparing Hume's remarks about necessary connections with his contrasting remarks about causal relations. His clearest statement of his position concerning necessary connections is given in this passage:

> The necessary connexion betwixt causes and effects is the foundation of our inference from one to the other. The foundation of our inference is the transition arising from the accustom'd union. They are, therefore, the same. (p. 165)

When Hume here speaks of the "foundation of our inference" from cause to effect, he cannot mean the warrant for this inference, for the skepticism concerning induction precludes any such warrant. He must, therefore, be speaking of a causal foundation and the passage goes on to say just this. Speaking carefully, our idea of necessity must be derived from an impression of this "transition arising from the accustom'd union." Hume thus goes on to say:

> Upon the whole, necessity is something, that exists in the mind, not in objects; nor is it possible for us ever to form the most distant idea of it, consider'd as a quality in bodies. Either we have no idea of necessity, or necessity is nothing but that determination of the thought to pass from causes to effects and from effects to causes, according to their experienc'd union. (pp. 165–6)

If we fail to see that Hume is here using causal notions to explicate the idea of a necessary connection and not proceeding in the reverse direction, we miss the point of his argument.

The passage just cited has another important feature: Hume no longer restricts his remarks to the necessary connection betwixt causes and effects, but, instead, speaks quite generally about necessity. This brings us to a passage that can serve as a proof text for any plausible interpretation of Hume's account of necessity:

Causality, Necessity, and Induction

> Thus as the necessity, which makes two times two equal to four, or three angles of a triangle equal to two right ones, lies only in the act of the understanding, by which we consider and compare these ideas; in like manner the necessity or power, which unites causes and effects, lies in the determination of the mind to pass from the one to the other. (p. 166)

Hume does not, as a positivist might, identify necessity with analyticity and then turn skeptical because he is unable to find any such necessity associated with causal relations. Hume does discover such an associated idea and then claims, contrary to positivism, that it is the very same idea of necessity involved in truths of reason. This does not mean that the distinction between truths of reason and truths gained from experience breaks down. The denial of a truth of reason is self-contradictory whereas the denial of a truth derived from experience is still always possible. It is simply a mistake, however, to associate the idea of necessity with the first category to the exclusion of the second. It is equally a mistake to think that necessity has a different significance in these two areas. In each case, the idea of necessity emerges from the impressions we have of the determinations – i.e., causal determinations – of the human mind.

All that remains to be shown is that Hume takes a very different line concerning causal relations. This is brought out in response to a criticism he poses for himself:

> What! the efficacy of causes lies in the determination of the mind! As if causes did not operate entirely independent of the mind, and wou'd not continue their operation, even tho' there was no mind existent to contemplate them, or reason concerning them. Thought may well depend on causes for its operation, but not causes on thought. (p. 167)

This complaint involves the very confusion that I have been trying to dispel, and this comes out clearly in Hume's reply:

> As to what may be said, that the operations of nature are independent of our thought and reasoning, I allow it; and accordingly have observ'd that objects bear to each other the relations of contiguity and succession; that like objects may be observ'd in several instances to have like relations; and all this is independent of, and antecedent to the operations of

the understanding. But if we go any farther, and ascribe a *power* or *necessary connexion* to these objects; this is what we can never observe in them, but must draw the idea of it from what we feel internally in contemplating them. (My italics, pp. 168–9)

Thus causal relations – whose definition Hume sketches in the first part of this passage – are one thing; necessary connections are something else.

This development has an important further consequence: it allows Hume to complete his analysis of causal relations. We may recall that when Hume first hit upon the idea of constant conjunction, he was largely dissatisfied with it: "to tell the truth, this new-discover'd relation of a constant conjunction seems to advance us but very little in our way, etc." (p. 88). At that point in the text, Hume is still thrashing about in a neighboring field searching for an account of necessity that will reveal it as the ground for causal inferences. My main argument so far is that after Hume presents his skeptical argument concerning induction he is able to relieve the idea of necessity of this justificatory role and can then complete his analysis of it. In support of this we can notice the final remark made by Hume just before he presents his skeptical argument: "Perhaps 'twill appear in the end, that the necessary connexion depends on the inference, instead of the inference's depending on the necessary connexion" (p. 88). This, of course, is how things do appear in the end. But now a burden has been lifted from a correct account of causal relations themselves: a reference to necessity need not form an essential part of their definition. This is borne out when we examine Hume's first definition of a CAUSE where it is treated as a philosophical relation:

> We may define a CAUSE to be 'An object precedent and contiguous to another, and where all the objects resembling the former are plac'd in like relations of precedency and contiguity to those objects, that resemble the latter.' (p. 170)

As noticed earlier, and contrary to Kemp Smith's claim, causation is here defined without reference to necessitation, determination, or agency. I think that it has become clear why a definition of this kind, though previously rejected, now can seem legitimate.

Causality, Necessity, and Induction

It might be useful to contrast the position developed here with that presented by J. L. Mackie in his *Cement of the Universe*. Mackie sees much the same development in the text that I have traced out, but his emphasis is different. He thinks that Hume, probably without realizing it, employs the notion of necessity in two distinct ways:

> We might call *necessity*$_1$ whatever is the distinguishing feature of causal as opposed to non-causal sequence, and *necessity*$_2$ the supposed warrant for an *a priori* inference, for example, the power which if we found it in C would tell us at once that C would bring about E, or some corresponding feature which if we found it in E would tell us at once that E had been produced by C, or some relation between one kind of thing and another which told us that things of those kinds could occur only in sequences, with a thing of the second kind following a thing of the first.[6]

Mackie holds that Hume is right in thinking that no idea can be found that will perform the role necessity$_2$, but that in no way shows that no idea can be found corresponding to necessity$_1$, i.e., that idea which would distinguish causal from non-causal sequences. Mackie concludes that Hume's "search for necessity$_1$ is sacrificed to his argument about necessity$_2$."[7]

Two things are worth noting. First, Hume connects the idea of a causal relation with that of an inference because, as we have seen, he holds that a causal relation and a causal relation alone provides the basis for an inference beyond immediate experience. It is for this reason that Hume associates causal relations with empirical inferences. At first – but not, as I have argued, in the end – Hume entertains the idea that what Mackie calls necessity$_2$ might yield a warrant for this inference. The need for Mackie's necessity$_2$ disappears with the skepticism with regard to induction.

With regard to Mackie's necessity$_1$, I don't think that Hume worries very long (or very much) about the difference between causal and non-causal sequences. At the beginning of his discussion he notices that in a *particular* case two events can be contiguous and prior without there being a causal relationship between them. Unable to find anything linking the events that would enable him to draw this distinction, he abandons the direct pursuit of his quarry and beats two neighboring fields. Eventually he comes to identify causality with a particular kind of *regular* sequence. Now starting with Reid, philosophers have persistently asked what distinguishes regular sequences that are causal from regular sequences that are non-causal.[8] As remarkable as this may seem, Hume never addressed himself to this particular problem, at least in his published works.

How could this be? One explanation is that the counter-examples to Hume's regularity definition, however obvious they may seem to us now, simply did not occur to him. This is probably right, but it merely raises another question. If Hume had tested his theory against various regularities, he certainly would have encountered Reid-like counter-examples; why then didn't he do so? I think that the best explanation for this is that Hume never argues *directly* for his regularity definition: in a manner of speaking, he backs into it. He begins with the tentative supposition that a causal sequence is a regular sequence of necessarily connected events. He then displaces the necessity from the sequence into the mind, leaving behind only regularity of sequence as the objective content of a causal sequence. Then, without looking back, he goes on to talk about other things he finds more important: the causes of our beliefs, including the causes of our causal beliefs. We can turn to this subject next.

V

SKEPTICISM AND THE TRIUMPH OF THE IMAGINATION

In the previous discussion I examined the relationship between Hume's skepticism concerning induction, his account of our idea of a necessary connection, and his first (or philosophical) definition of a causal relation. Here I shall examine another development in the text which is, if anything, more important for following the main lines of Hume's thought: his use of inductive skepticism to elevate the standing of the *imagination*.

At the beginning of Section V, Hume outlines the task that will occupy him for the nine sections that constitute the heart of Part III of Book I:

> All our arguments concerning causes and effects consist both of an impression of the memory or senses, and of the idea of that existence, which produces the object of the impression, or is produc'd by it. Here therefore we have three things to explain, *viz. First*, The original impression. *Secondly*, The transition to the idea of the connected cause or effect. *Thirdly*, The nature and qualities of that idea. (p. 84)

In the first part of this program, Hume presents his theory of belief, telling us that "*belief* or *assent*, which always attends the memory and senses, is *nothing but* the vivacity of these perceptions they present; and that this alone distinguishes them from the imagination" (emphasis added, p. 86). There are few portions of the *Treatise* less coherently developed, for Hume seems unable to decide between two theses:

Skepticism and the Triumph of the Imagination

(i) Vivacity is definitive of the difference between sense and memory on one hand, and imagination on the other.
(ii) It is simply a nearly universal fact that perceptions of sense and memory are vivacious, whereas, perceptions of imagination are not.[1]

More perplexing still, Hume seems to suggest that perceptions generated by the imagination only rarely acquire a vivacity or force amounting to belief. This, however, is not a true reflection of his position, at least if the imagination is understood in the broad sense in which Hume commonly speaks of it. As we shall see, imagination supplies the idea of the unobserved cause (or effect) upon the occurrence of an experienced effect (or cause) in memory or sense. Without the imagination, we would be forever trapped in the solipsism of sense and recollection. The plain man's belief in the continued and distinct existence of what he perceives is also grounded in the imagination, as are the beliefs that arise from philosophical reflection. Far from being exceptional, the vivification of perceptions of the imagination to the status of beliefs is a common feature of our experiences involved in daily life, scientific inquiry, and philosophical reflection.[2]

But even if our minds are largely filled with the vivified products of the imagination, perceptions of sense and memory maintain an important priority over the perceptions of the imagination. A perception of sense or memory "constitutes the first act of the judgment, and lays the foundation of that reasoning, which we build upon it, when we trace the relation of cause and effect" (p. 86). Earlier in the *Treatise*, Hume maintained that impressions provide the basic *content* for all other perceptions. Though he trumpets this empiricist doctrine, as far as I can see it plays largely a secondary (and mostly negative) role in the development of the central themes of his philosophy.[3] In the present context, impressions of sense enter into Hume's mental economy in quite a different way. Even if we could have ideas whose constituents had no origin in immediate experience, none of these ideas could be beliefs in the absence of this "first act of judgment" given in impressions of sense. We might call this aspect of Hume's position his *doxastic empiricism*. It is, I believe, more important than his

Skepticism and the Triumph of the Imagination

conceptual empiricism for the development of the main features of his naturalistic program.

Returning to the central argument of the text, in acquiring a causal belief, we (i) begin with a vivid perception, (ii) make a transition to a new perception, and (iii) then this new perception is vivified. Examining the transition presented in the second part of this process brings us once more to Hume's skeptical argument concerning induction. This time, however, we will view it in a different light: instead of concentrating upon the soundness of various *arguments* that might be offered in justification of causal inferences, we will show how Hume presents his skeptical argument to settle a competition between two *faculties*, the understanding and the imagination.

> Since it appears, that the transition from an impression present to the memory or senses to the idea of an object, which we call cause or effect, is founded on past *experience,* and on our remembrance of their *constant conjunction,* the next question is, Whether experience produces the idea by means of the understanding or of the imagination; whether we are determin'd by reason to make the transition, or by a certain association and relation of perceptions. (pp. 88–9)

That is, given the fact that the transition from a present impression to an associated idea is "founded on past experience," Hume here asks whether the faculty of the understanding or the faculty of the imagination utilizes this experience to produce this new idea. Hume's skepticism concerning induction is explicitly introduced to show that the understanding is incapable of performing this task. In the language of the first *Enquiry*, Hume's inductive skepticism is intended to raise doubts "concerning the operations of the understanding."

Of course, the elimination of the understanding from the competition does not show at once that the transition in question is grounded in principles of the imagination. Hume sees this and completes his argument (perhaps too quickly) in these words:

> We have already taken notice of certain relations, which make us pass from one object to another, even tho' there be no reason to determine us to that transition; and this we may establish for a general rule, that wherever the mind

Skepticism and the Triumph of the Imagination

> constantly and uniformly makes a transition without any reason, it is influenc'd by these relations. Now this is exactly the present case. Reason can never shew us the connexion of one object with another, tho' aided by experience, and the observation of their constant conjunction in all past experience. When the mind, therefore, passes from the idea or impression of one object to the idea or belief of another, it is not determin'd by reason, but by certain principles, which associate together the ideas of these objects, and unite them in the imagination. (p. 92)

This, I believe, is the central argument of Book I, Part III. What we now call Hume's skepticism concerning induction, for all its independent importance, occurs as a step leading to the conclusion that causal inferences (so called) are the product of the imagination and not of any kind of reasoning.

Now that Hume has explained the transition from impression to idea, he need only explain how the idea acquires the status of a belief in order to complete his project. He answers this with his doctrine of vivacity transfer:

> I wou'd willingly establish it as a general maxim in the science of human nature, *that when any impression becomes present to us, it not only transports the mind to such ideas as are related to it, but likewise communicates to them a share of its force and vivacity.* (p. 98)

Since no other faculty presents itself as a candidate, this too seems to describe an activity of the imagination.

Read one way, this passage has a peculiar consequence. Hume speaks of the impression *communicating a share* of its vivacity to the related ideas, and this suggests that it must give up some of its vivacity and thus be somewhat less strongly believed. I am sure that Hume did not intend this result. The passage also suggests that the related idea may receive only a share of the impression's vivacity, i.e., it will not (or, at least, need not) have the same degree of vivacity as the original impression. Now there is no reason for Hume to resist this result, for it often happens that we have more confidence in the existence of the event that is taking place before our eyes than in the existence of any event that we infer from it. Hume further holds that the related idea will never

Skepticism and the Triumph of the Imagination

have more, but may sometimes have less, vivacity than the original impression. In fact, however, he maintains an even stronger thesis: when an impression's vivacity is shared by a number of related ideas, then the total amount of vivacity inherited by these related ideas cannot exceed the original *quantum* of vivacity in the original impression.

Hume uses these principles to answer a difficult criticism he poses for himself in Section IX: if the imagination is guided by three principles of association, why don't the relations of *contiguity* and *resemblance* generate beliefs in the same way that the relation of cause and effect does? Hume's answer is that these relations *do* have a tendency to reinforce beliefs.

> To begin with contiguity; it has been remark'd among the *Mahometans* as well as *Christians*, that those *pilgrims*, who have seen MECCA or the HOLY LAND are ever after more faithful and zealous believers, than those who have not had that advantage. (p. 110)

Hume makes a similar point about *resemblance*. In fact, Hume goes to great length to explain the origin of those beliefs that lack a proper foundation in causal reasoning. The very magnificence of our imagined idea may lend it a forcefulness that commands our assent. We are also naturally inclined to accept the testimony of others, and although this has a basis in past experience, "[we] have a remarkable propensity to believe whatever is reported, even concerning apparitions, enchantments, and prodigies, however contrary to daily experience and observation" (p. 113). And ideas constantly implanted in the imagination through education can acquire the force of belief (see pp. 116ff.). Hume cites all these examples as further evidence for his definition of belief. When a perception of the imagination acquires a proper degree of vivacity *by whatever means*, it is then believed or perhaps *is* a belief. Hume's insistence on this point does not go against his central thesis that a belief is a lively idea related to or associated with a *present* impression. He is insisting that this relation or association can be other than causal.

Granting all this, pride of place still goes to association by way of causal relations:

> But tho' I cannot altogether exclude the relations of

Skepticism and the Triumph of the Imagination

> resemblance and contiguity from operating on the fancy in this manner, 'tis observable that, when single, their influence is very feeble and uncertain. As the relation of cause and effect is requisite to persuade us of any real existence, so is this persuasion requisite to give force to these other relations. (p. 109)

Here Hume's approach is part descriptive and, as we shall see in a moment, part normative. Descriptively, transitions in terms of contiguity and resemblance are not tied down in a determinate way. Given one idea, the mind is free to pass to any number of other ideas that resemble it, and the same is true for associations *via* contiguity.

> There is no manner of necessity for the mind to feign any resembling and contiguous objects; and if it feigns such, there is as little necessity for it always to confine itself to the same, without any difference or variation. (p. 109)

"The relation of cause and effect," Hume says, "has all the opposite advantages":

> The thought is always determin'd to pass from the impression to the idea, and from that particular impression to that particular idea, without any choice or hesitation. (p. 110)

Hume thus invokes a kind of "wage pool" principle for the dispersal of vivacity: there is only so much vivacity to be portioned out between associated ideas. Resemblance and contiguity present a vast range of possible associations and therefore the quantum of vivacity passed on to any particular associated idea is correspondingly small. The reverse, he argues, is true of associations *via* cause and effect: the transition is tied down in a particular way, and, not being squandered, all the vivacity accrues to an individual idea.

The most striking use of this economic (or wage pool) theory of vivacity distribution occurs in Hume's development of a subjective theory of probability.[4] Again we are dealing with a case where the vivacity of a given impression is distributed over a number of related ideas, but now, in order to make his theory work, Hume assumes that the quantum of distributed vivacity must actually *equal* the quantum of vivacity in the original impression. Given

Skepticism and the Triumph of the Imagination

this principle, Hume goes on to explain *a priori* probabilities (what he calls probability of *chances*) in the following way: Consider a die with a single dot on four sides and double dots on the remaining two. From past experience I come to believe that any side is as likely as any other to come up. With respect to the sides of the die I am in a state of indifference, i.e., I am not inclined to believe *more strongly* that one side will come up rather than any other. But now the imagination enters the scene in a new and constructive manner: various outcomes are coalesced and considered as a single outcome. I thus reflect upon the chance that a side with a single dot will come up and contrast this with the chance that two dots will come up. With this move, the vivacity of the individual cases is also coalesced, and I come to believe twice as strongly that a single dot will appear than that a double dot will appear.

Again, it is important to stress the interplay between imagination and belief. As always, it is the imagination that produces the new object for belief, but here the object is, in a sense, different in kind. Put crudely, I transcend four $1/6$th beliefs to a single $2/3$rds belief. But we have to be careful here not to depart from Hume's theory of abstract ideas. When I think of a single dot coming up, I have in mind a particular event, even though I employ this idea to represent a plurality of events:

> Abstract ideas are therefore in themselves individual, however
> they may become general in their representation. The image
> in the mind is only that of a particular object, tho' the
> application of it in our reasoning be the same, as if it were
> universal. (p. 20)

When one idea acts as the representative for others of the same kind it acquires their portion of vivacity. At least I think that this is how Hume would relate his theory of abstract ideas to his theory of subjective probability.

Hume's account of the probability of *causes* is much the same as his account of the probability of *chances*. They seem to differ in this way: the probability of *chance* depends upon an enumeration of equally likely outcomes. This demands an appeal to experience. Beyond this, however, imagination steps in and, by combining various outcomes, yields a degree of belief proportioned to the ratio of one kind of case to the total number of

Skepticism and the Triumph of the Imagination

cases. In this way, the notion of an *a priori* probability calculus is mirrored in Hume's naturalistic system. In contrast, the degree of belief that arises for the probability of causes is conditioned upon the experienced ratio of actual – not imagined – cases. If we have experienced a regularity holding to a certain extent in the past, we then project this same degree of regularity into the future. Beyond this, in the *particular* case, the strength of our belief is a function of the extent of this past regularity. In this way, Hume can assign a statistical probability to a single event.[5]

Before leaving the topic of probability, I wish to examine an important aspect of Hume's theory that has been almost totally neglected: his discussion of so called *unphilosophical probability* in Section XIII. In recent years cognitive psychologists have studied the curious phenomenon that subjective probability assignments are often at variance – sometimes widely – with values we would assign using standard *a priori* or statistical procedures.[6] Hume saw this as well, and invoked his theory of belief to explain this phenomenon. He offers four main reasons for this discrepancy between philosophical and unphilosophical probabilities. An argument that convinced in the past may lose some of its force as the vivacity of the original impressions it relied upon fade as memories (p. 143). Just as we do not give old evidence the weight it deserves, we tend to overvalue the evidence fresh in memory (p. 143). Vivacity tends to fade if we attempt to carry it over long chains of inferences (p. 144). Finally, we have a strong tendency to follow "*general rules*, which we rashly form to ourselves, and which are the source of what we properly call PREJUDICE" (pp. 146ff.).

Hume dwells particularly on the fourth circumstance and his reflections lead him to a radical conclusion that foreshadows some of the extreme developments in Part IV of Book I. He cites our views concerning national character as an instance of our tendency to cling to rashly formed general rules.

> An *Irishman* cannot have wit, and a *Frenchman* cannot have solidity; for which reason, tho' the conversation of the former in any instance be visibly very agreeable, and of the latter very judicious, we have entertain'd such a prejudice against them, that they must be dunces or fops in spite of sense and reason. (pp. 146–7)

Skepticism and the Triumph of the Imagination

There are two reasons why reliance on general rules can mislead us: (1) we often form them rashly, i.e., on the basis of too small a sample and (2) even when they are well grounded, we have a tendency to use them beyond their range of proper application:

> The same custom goes beyond the instances, from which it is deriv'd, and to which it perfectly corresponds; and influences [one's] ideas of such objects as are in some respect resembling, but fall not precisely under the same rule. (p. 148)

Hume repeats this claim much later in the *Treatise*:

> For there is a principle of human nature, which we have frequently taken notice of, that men are mightily addicted to *general rules*, and that we often carry our maxims beyond those reasons, which first induc'd us to establish them. (p. 551)

It is natural to read this discussion as a set of *warnings* about the way in which we can go wrong in our probabilistic reasoning. In part this is right, for Hume does include a section enumerating a set of *rules by which to judge of causes and effects* (pp. 173ff.). More deeply, this discussion provides the first occasion where Hume speaks of various operations of the human understanding coming into opposition with one another. Why, we might ask, do "men form general rules, and allow them to influence their judgment, even contrary to present observation and experience"? (p. 147). Hume responds:

> in my opinion it proceeds from those very principles, on which all judgments concerning causes and effects depend. Our judgments concerning cause and effect are deriv'd from habit and experience; and when we have been accustom'd to see one object united to another, our imagination passes from the first to the second, *by a natural transition, which precedes reflection, and which cannot be prevented by it*. (Emphasis added, p. 147)

To this Hume adds even the stronger claim that

> tho' custom be the foundation of all our judgments, yet sometimes it has an effect on the imagination in opposition to the judgment, and produces a contrariety in our sentiments concerning the same object. (pp. 147–8)

Skepticism and the Triumph of the Imagination

At this point a dialectical conflict emerges. The imagination underlies all our causal reasoning, yet, at the same time, it can generate beliefs in opposition to our causal reasoning. What we *say* in such circumstances is that our well-founded general rules are the product of the understanding, whereas beliefs formed more capriciously are the product of the imagination. This, however, is merely a nominal answer, for both sorts of belief arise naturally from the imagination, and, given the skepticism with regard to induction, we have no independent grounds for preferring one to the other. Hume immediately draws a skeptical conclusion from this conflict between these two products of the imagination.

> Mean while the sceptics may here have the pleasure of observing a new and signal contradiction in our reason, and of seeing all philosophy ready to be subverted by a principle of human nature, and again sav'd by a new direction of the very same principle. The following of general rules is a very unphilosophical species of probability; and yet 'tis only by following them that we can correct this, and all other unphilosophical probabilities. (p. 150)

It may not be immediately clear what the skeptic is so pleased about. The key, I think, is Hume's reference to following a general rule as a *species* of probability. By this I think he means that the mere act of bringing a future prospect under a general rule will endow it with a some degree of acceptance even when the subsumption is to some degree arbitrary.[7] The contradiction, and it is rather lame by Humean standards, comes to this: our propensity to rely on general rules often leads us into error, so we shouldn't rely on general rules, but this very pronouncement is yet another instance of yielding to this propensity, so in the very act of rejecting general rules, we embrace one. Here Hume over-reaches.

At this stage of the *Treatise*, Hume's position seems to come to this: although our instinctive perseverance in general rules may sometimes lead us into error, following them usually amounts to a good strategy in dealing with the world around us and with the people in it. To anticipate the future, we must not only assume that nature and human conduct are largely uniform, but also that the information that comes our way is reasonably representative

Skepticism and the Triumph of the Imagination

of these uniformities. For Hume, these "assumptions" are built into the fabric of the human understanding. This mental machinery could have been more finely tuned. We could have been so constituted to appreciate differences more and similarities less. The upshot would be that we would arrive more slowly at fewer, but more accurate, general rules. Carried to an extreme, however, such diffidence in accepting general rules would deprive us of the rules of common sense necessary for the preservation of life. Nature, it seems, has taken a middle way, accepting a certain amount of inevitable falsehood as a reasonable price to pay for efficiency.[8]

Later in the *Treatise*, Hume seems to take a different and more startling attitude toward falsehoods generated by our tendency to form uncritical commitments to general rules: in his discussion of the artificial virtues, he seems to suggest that a commitment to such falsehoods is, in fact, essential for society's upholding its conventions. Furthermore, adherence to general rules is not the only source of pervasive and sometimes fortunate falsehood. These falsehoods include virtually all of our perceptual and moral judgments. The endemic falsehood of the plain man's perceptual judgments is the subject of the next chapter. The remarkably similar treatment of moral judgments is discussed in Chapter X.

VI

SKEPTICISM WITH REGARD TO THE SENSES

This title marks one of the most perplexing portions of the *Treatise*. Even the title is perplexing since, for the most part, Hume does not forward skeptical arguments against our perceptual faculties. He argues instead that the experimental method of reasoning reveals that the vast majority of our common perceptual judgments are simply false. These falsehoods are endemic, grounded in the framework of our faculties, and they press themselves upon us as soon as we relax our philosophical attention. Included in this class of shared perceptual falsehoods are the beliefs that we are aware of common public objects (rather than of our own private perceptions), that these things of which we are aware can have a continued and distinct existence outside the mind, and that these things exhibit an identity over time and a genuine unity at a given time.

To the extent that Hume argues that these beliefs are false, he is not, of course, a skeptic. He is not a theoretical skeptic, because he claims to know the truth on these matters. More strikingly, he does not recommend a wholesale abandonment of these falsehoods in favor of the truths he and most other modern philosophers acknowledge. A scientific inquiry into the operations of the human mind must be guided by a proper understanding of these matters, but there is no need to carry this over to daily life. Though we are thoroughly convinced by the teaching of modern philosophy that the flavor of a fig is not resident in that object, that is the way it strikes us, and, when not doing philosophy,

Skepticism with Regard to the Senses

that is what we believe. The same holds for the other common falsehoods enumerated above.

Furthermore, Hume does not deplore this fact that our common perceptual judgments are everywhere infected with falsehood. In the first place, these falsehoods, since almost universally shared, cause little, if any, confusion. Although we all go wrong, we all go wrong in pretty much the same ways. Beyond this, Hume often suggests that we are fortunate that nature has endowed humans with this propensity to generate commonly shared falsehoods. If our existence depended upon penetrating the inner workings of nature, our case would be hopeless. Nature has found it more efficient to provide us with a rich and useful system of false beliefs, rather than trusting our existence to the scattering of truths that our meager intellect might supply.

It is not difficult to recognize the relationship between this aspect of Hume's philosophy and his naturalistic program. The discovery that most of our perceptual beliefs are false is, in the first place, the *result* of empirical investigations. It is the result of observation of phenomena and experiments concerning them. This discovery also provides one of the central *tasks* of Hume's program: the explanation of the origin of these shared falsehoods through the regular principles of the mind that generate them.

But if Hume is not a skeptic concerning the plain man's (false) perceptual judgments, he is a skeptic – and an unmitigated skeptic of a traditional kind – with respect to the *philosopher*'s attempt to gain knowledge beyond the perceptually given. This difference is alluded to by Hume at the beginning of this section where, speaking of the skeptic, he remarks that "he must assent to the principle concerning the existence of body, tho' he cannot pretend by any arguments of philosophy to maintain its veracity" (p. 187). The impossibility of a proof in this area provides Hume with a reason for limiting the scope of his investigation:

> We may well ask, *What causes induce us to believe in the existence of body?* but 'tis in vain to ask, *Whether there be body or not?* That is a point, which we must take for granted in all our reasonings. (p. 187)

The final sentence admits of a double reading that reflects the two sides of Hume's position. We must take the existence of body for

Skepticism with Regard to the Senses

granted, first, because it is incapable of proof and, second, because we are incapable of doubting it. Now it is important not to let this second point bury the first, for Hume is unequivocal in accepting the force of the standard skeptical arguments against the possibility of proving the existence of external bodies. This becomes evident toward the end of the section where he argues that only causal reasoning could assure us of the existence of bodies, but this, since we never observe bodies conjoined with perceptions, is impossible.

> 'Tis impossible . . . that from the existence or any of the qualities of the former [i.e., perceptions], we can ever form any conclusion concerning the existence of the latter [i.e., objects], or ever satisfy our reason in this particular. (p. 212)

Speaking of this same argument in the *Enquiry*, Hume tells us that

> this is a topic . . . in which the profounder and more philosophical sceptics will always triumph, when they endeavour to introduce an universal doubt into all subjects of human knowledge and enquiry. (*E.*, p. 153)

The arguments of these *profounder and more philosophical sceptics* are not sophisms easily resolved; they are, in fact, irrefutable.

Thus it is important to sort things out by distinguishing between Hume's treatment of the plain man's perceptual beliefs and his treatment of the philosopher's attempt to improve upon them.

(i) Hume holds that virtually all the plain man's perceptual judgments are false. The discussion entitled "Of scepticism with regard to the senses" is largely (though not exclusively) concerned with giving a causal account of the origins of these false beliefs.

(ii) But Hume further holds that the philosopher's efforts to replace the plain man's naive position with something better are subject to irrefutable skeptical attacks. Hume attempts to give a causal account of the philosopher's propensity to generate and, incredibly enough, accept certain traditional views concerning perception.

In this chapter I shall examine Hume's treatment of the perceptual

Skepticism with Regard to the Senses

beliefs of the vulgar.[1] In the next chapter I shall discuss his treatment of the philosopher's views on these matters.

What does a person believe when he believes in the existence of body? The foundation for answering this question is laid earlier in the *Treatise* where Hume discusses our ideas of existence and external existence. With respect to external existence, Hume says this:

> We may observe, that 'tis universally allow'd by philosophers, and is besides pretty obvious of itself, that nothing is ever really present with the mind but its perceptions or impressions and ideas, and that external objects become known to us only by those perceptions they occasion. To hate, to love, to think, to feel, to see; all this is nothing but to perceive. (p. 67)

The most natural reading of this passage – or, at least, the first sentence of this passage – suggests a causal theory of perception. There are external objects and there are perceptions: external objects are only known by the perceptions they occasion. Yet Hume quickly moves away from any such double existence theory and later explicitly rejects it.[2] The above passage continues as follows:

> Now since nothing is ever present to the mind but perceptions, and since all ideas are deriv'd from something antecedently present to the mind; it follows, that *'tis impossible for us so much as to conceive or form an idea of any thing specifically different from ideas and impressions.* (My italics, p. 67)

In sum, if we are going to give an account of our belief in external existence, we cannot hold that this belief concerns things different in kind (specifically different) from perceptions. The mind has no capacity to raise up such ideas.

If Hume were content to let matters rest here, we would have an example of pure conceptual skepticism. If by an external object we mean something different in kind from a perception, postulating external objects as the cause or occasion of our perceptions would be an hypothesis with no content. Taken this way, the words "external existence" will have no idea corresponding to them. But this is not Hume's position, or, at least, not his whole position. Men commonly believe in external existence, and

Skepticism with Regard to the Senses

that belief stands in need of explanation. All we know so far is that one account of this belief – that bodies are entities *specifically* different from perceptions – makes no sense. This leads Hume to adopt something like a phenomenalist position; our belief in the existence of body does not rest upon a relationship between perceptions and non-perceptions; it is grounded in a system of relationships among perceptions.[3]

The second important step in Hume's argument occurs almost at once: In our belief in an external existence (or, alternatively, in a body), we

> attribute a CONTINU'D existence to objects, even when they are not present to the senses; and . . . we suppose them to have an existence DISTINCT from the mind and perception. (p. 188)

For Hume, understanding the causes of our belief in external existence amounts to understanding the causes for these two attributions.

To follow the development in the text, Hume asks in turn, whether sense, reason, or imagination gives rise to our idea of a continued and distinct existence. The summary passage concerning the senses reads as follows:

> they give us no notion of continu'd existence, because they cannot operate beyond the extent, in which they really operate. They as little produce the opinion of a distinct existence, because they neither can offer it to the mind as represented, nor as original. To offer it as represented, they must present both an object and an image. To make it appear as original, they must convey a falsehood; and this falsehood must lie in the relations and situation: In order to which they must be able to compare the object with ourselves; and even in that case they do not, nor is it possible they shou'd, deceive us. We may, therefore, conclude with certainty, that the opinion of a continu'd and of a distinct existence never arises from the senses. (pp. 191–2)

Hume's first point is trivially correct: the senses cannot convey the idea of a *continued* unsensed existence, since this would involve sensing the unsensed. The further argument showing that the senses cannot convey the idea of a *distinct* existence has the

Skepticism with Regard to the Senses

form of a dilemma. The idea in question must be either *representational* or *original*. Our senses cannot show us that our perceptions are representational. When I perceive this lamp, I am not aware of two things – a perception and the object it represents. No such representational relationship is found within sense. The second horn of Hume's dilemma is dealt with more obscurely. If we had an original idea of a distinct existence, then the senses themselves would inform us that the thing of which I am aware has a distinct existence. Yet such a belief is false, so Hume goes on to say: "If our senses, therefore, suggest any idea of distinct existences, they must convey the impressions as those very existences, by a kind of fallacy and illusion" (p. 189). But this he says is impossible, since:

> Every thing that enters the mind, being in *reality* a perception, 'tis impossible any thing shou'd to *feeling* appear different.
> This were to suppose, that even where we are most intimately conscious, we might be mistaken. (p. 190)

It is not clear to me what the second sentence means.

Reason's candidacy as the source of our belief in continued and distinct existence of objects is dismissed in a single paragraph. Hume first argues genetically. Even supposing that there were such arguments, they must be known "but to very few, and that 'tis not by them, that children, peasants, and the greatest part of mankind are induc'd to attribute objects to some impressions, and deny them to others" (p. 193). More strongly, philosophical reflection convinces us, again, that the belief of the vulgar is false: "For philosophy informs us, that every thing, which appears to the mind, is nothing but a perception, and is interrupted, and dependent on the mind . . ." (p. 193).

Given Hume's inventory of mental faculties, we are left with only the imagination as the source of this "entirely unreasonable sentiment." Imagination is, of course, a natural candidate for supplying the content of a false belief. Through the imagination we can construct an idea of a hippogriff or a chickopotamus even though no such things exist. Beyond this, ideas of the imagination sometimes, at least, become ideas that we believe. Broadly speaking, Hume is thus faced with two tasks: (i) to explain how the imagination can concoct the idea of a perception with a continued and distinct existence, and (ii) to explain how belief can reside in "so extraordinary an opinion" (p. 195).

Skepticism with Regard to the Senses

Hume first gives an informal exposition of his position and then repeats his discussion in a more rigorous way. He first remarks that we do not attribute a continued and distinct existence to all of our perceptions. Though vivid and not subject to our voluntary control, we do not attribute a continued distinct existence to pains and passions.[4] Only objects that have a certain constancy or coherence in their appearance are thought to have a continued and distinct existence. This much Hume presents as a statement of fact, but the question remains *why* we make such attributions. He answers that the mind moves most *naturally* when it is confronted with a series of perceptions that are either constant or coherent. An encounter with inconstancy or incoherence will jar it from its natural course. Yet the mind has a tendency to persevere in its natural course just as "a galley put in motion by the oars, carries on its course without any new impulse" (p. 198). Invoking this analogy with the principle of inertia, Hume goes on to say:

> Objects have a certain coherence even as they appear to our senses; but this coherence is much greater and more uniform, if we suppose the objects to have a continu'd existence; and as the mind is once in the train of observing an uniformity among objects, it naturally continues, till it renders the uniformity as compleat as possible. The simple supposition of their continu'd existence suffices for this purpose, and gives us a notion of a much greater regularity among objects, than what they have when we look no farther than our senses.
> (p. 198)

Here Hume is speaking about coherence, but he goes on to indicate that it is really constancy that is the chief source of our idea of a continued and distinct existence. But this difference need not detain us and we can notice his concluding remark on this subject:

> This inference from the constancy of our perceptions, like the precedent from their coherence, gives rise to the opinion of the *continu'd* existence of body, which is prior to that of its *distinct* existence, and produces that latter principle.
> (p. 199)

The transition to a more profound level of analysis is marked by the introduction of a new notion:

Skepticism with Regard to the Senses

> [When] the perception of the sun or ocean, for instance, returns upon us after an absence or annihilation with like parts and in a like order, as at its first appearance, we are not apt to regard these interrupted perceptions as different, (*which they really are*) but on the contrary consider them as individually the same, upon account of their resemblance. (My italics, p. 199)

That is, my assumption that the thing I perceive now is related by a continued existence to something I perceived earlier involves the false claim that what I observe now is identical with what I observed earlier. Thus, to complete his analysis, Hume must explain the nature and origin of our idea of *identity*.

Hume poses his question concerning identity in the form of a dilemma: "the view of any one object is not sufficient to convey the idea of identity," and "a multiplicity of objects can never convey this idea, however resembling they may be suppos'd" (p. 200). The first view, Hume says, rather obscurely, conveys the idea of *unity*, the second view the idea of *number*.[5] He then claims to be baffled, at least for the moment:

> Since then both number and unity are incompatible with the relation of identity, it must lie in something that is neither of them. But to tell the truth, at first sight this seems utterly impossible. Betwixt unity and number there can be no medium; no more than betwixt existence and non-existence. (p. 200)

As we shall see in a moment, it will be hard to say whether Hume does find a medium betwixt unity and number – or even that he pretends to.

Not surprisingly, Hume has recourse to our idea of time or duration to solve this problem and here Hume's specific theory of the nature of time exerts an important influence on the discussion. Time, as Hume explained earlier in the *Treatise*, concerns the *manner* in which things change. A world with no change would have no time and, more specifically, an unchanging object can be said to be in time "only by a fiction of the imagination" (pp. 200–1). In a remarkable two-step argument, Hume will first explain how this fiction arises and will then use this fiction to explain our false belief that the relation of identity holds between distinct perceptions over time.

Skepticism with Regard to the Senses

Hume's argument proceeds in the following way: given an unchanging sequence of perceptions *in isolation* no conception of time arises. As far as our perception goes, we would be presented with a unitary object at a single moment of time. But suppose we consider this unchanging sequence of perceptions in conjunction with a simultaneous sequence that is changing qualitatively:

First Sequence	Second Sequence
A	A
A	B
A	C
A	D
A	E

The second sequence, of course, does not give us an idea of identity either, only multiplicity, but it does give us the idea of time or duration missing from the first sequence. Now Hume makes the ingenious suggestion that if we view the first sequence from the perspective of the second, then a multiplicity emerges in the first sequence as well. This is the genesis of the *fiction* that time exists where there is no change. Taken by itself, the first sequence reveals only a timeless unity, but measured against the second sequence it appears as a temporal sequence of similar perceptions. We thus arrive at Hume's account of our origin of the idea of *identity*:

> Here then is an idea, which is a medium betwixt unity and number; or more properly speaking, is either of them, according to the view, in which we take it: And this idea we call that of identity. (p. 201)

I find this passage completely baffling. The portion before the semicolon says one thing; the next bit takes it back; and the portion after the colon makes sense only in relation to the part that was rejected. Let me explain. Hume first says that he has found an idea that is a medium betwixt unity and number. We might read the passage this way: as the mind oscillates back and forth between two ideas, a new distinct idea comes into existence. Analogically, a card has one color on its front and another color on its back; the card is turned rapidly and a new color distinct

Skepticism with Regard to the Senses

from the other two appears. Somewhat differently, on one side of the card is a picture of a bird; on the other side the picture of a cage; the card is twirled and the bird appears to be in the cage. In the first case, a new *simple* impression is produced whereas in the second case a new *complex* impression arises. If Hume's account is at least *something* like this – my examples should not be taken literally – then we have some idea of how a new impression can come into existence by the mind acting like a thaumatrope.[6]

But in speaking "more properly" Hume suggests that nothing like this takes place; that is, *no* new idea emerges. We are still left with two ideas, unity and number, and an ability to attend to one or the other. If Hume is speaking very strictly, he must mean that identity is sometimes unity, sometimes number, but never both. It is not some wholly new idea arising from the activity of mind, as necessity was, nor is it some complex idea compounded of others as causation was. Speaking properly, it is no distinct idea at all. Yet Hume concludes by saying, "And this idea we call that of identity."

Deciding whether Hume thinks he has found an idea of identity or has not is essential for the following argument. It is only on the assumption that he has found such an idea that he has a right to speak of it as a *fiction* and go on to say that our attribution of identity to things (a sequence of perceptions) is *false*. In contrast, if he thinks it is a fiction to think that *we have* such an idea, the attribution, far from being false, is no attribution at all. The second, I think, is Hume's deepest solution to the problem he has posed for himself, but the first view dominates the text both before and after the passage I have cited. It seems that here, at least, Hume has developed a profound conceptual skepticism but has not thought through its consequences.

Anyway, we can go forward only on the assumption that Hume has the idea of identity in hand. Notice how he explains the second part of his system:

> I now proceed to explain the *second* part of my system, and shew why the constancy of our perceptions makes us ascribe to them a perfect numerical identity, tho' there be very long intervals betwixt their appearance, and they have only one

Skepticism with Regard to the Senses

of the essential qualities of identity, *viz. invariableness*. (pp. 201–2)

The discussion here gives a nice turn to the previous less formal explication. Suppose we compare the three sequences:

ABCDEFGH

AAAAAAAA

A__AAA__AA

An experience of the first two sequences leads to the fictitious belief in identity of an unchanging series of As over time. Yet we go on to apply this same fiction to the As in the interrupted sequence simply in virtue of an invariableness that it shares with the second sequence. But why are we not impressed with the obvious dissimilarity, i.e., the gaps? Why doesn't the presence of the gaps prevent us from falling into the error of ascribing numerical identity to the items in the interrupted sequence? We have made a mistake in assigning numerical identity to the items in the second sequence, and now in the third sequence this mistake should become obvious to us.

To answer this question, Hume extends his basic system in an important way: where previously he spoke only of the association of *ideas*, he now speaks of the association of *dispositions*:

> we may establish it for a general rule, that whatever ideas place the mind in the same disposition or in similar ones, are very apt to be confounded. The mind readily passes from one to the other, and perceives not the change without a strict attention, of which, generally speaking, 'tis wholly incapable. (p. 203)[7]

As might be expected, Hume argues that this very invariability common to the two sequences places the mind in the same disposition, and this lays the basis for the mistake (and it is a second mistake) of attributing numerical identity to the items in the interrupted sequence.

> An easy transition or passage of the imagination, along the ideas of these different and interrupted perceptions, is almost

Skepticism with Regard to the Senses

the same disposition of mind with that in which we consider
one constant and uninterrupted perception. 'Tis therefore
very natural for us to mistake the one for the other. (p. 204)

Notice that it is these two *dispositions* that are confounded, not the sequences themselves. Hume underscores this point in a footnote appended to this passage.

It is important to insist upon this last point because it sets the problem for the third part of Hume's system: his account of the "fiction of continu'd existence" (p. 205). The common disposition (or, at least, very similar disposition) produced by surveying the invariable uninterrupted and the invariable interrupted sequence leads us to assign numerical identity to the items in the interrupted sequence, but the actual appearance of gaps leads us to withdraw this assignment. "The perplexity arising from this contradiction produces a propension to unite these broken appearances by the fiction of a continu'd existence" (p. 205). We thus encounter a situation characteristic of Hume's philosophy: two mental faculties acting in opposition to one another. *Via* an underlying association of dispositions we have a propensity to attribute a numerical identity to the items in an interrupted sequence, and *via* immediate inspection of the sequence we have a propensity to deny this attribution. When a similar conflict of propensities occurred in Hume's skepticism concerning reason, Hume solved his problem by claiming that one propensity ultimately gives way: forced into unfamiliar territory, reason finally flags. Hume's answer here is different: both propensities are satisfied *via* a *fiction*. And a fiction seems appropriate in this case if we remember that Hume is here trying to explain the genesis of a *false* belief.

This last remark brings us to an important and difficult issue: isn't the belief in the continued existence of perceptions not just false but actually self-contradictory? Hume addresses this point directly:

as the *appearance* of a perception in the mind and its *existence*
seem at first sight entirely the same, it may be doubted,
whether we can ever assent to so palpable a contradiction,
and suppose a perception to exist without being present to
the mind. (p. 206)

Skepticism with Regard to the Senses

The passage contains a transparent reference to Berkeley, but the relationship here is complex. Although there is a change in terminology, Hume is following Berkeley when he says "that everything, which appears to the mind, is nothing but a perception . . . and dependent upon the mind" (p. 193). From this, Berkeley immediately concludes that it is a manifest contradiction to suppose that "sensible objects, have an existence, natural or real, distinct from their being perceived by the understanding." "Their *esse*," as he notoriously remarks, "is *percipe*." For Berkeley, "the *absolute* existence of unthinking things, without any relation to their being perceived is . . . perfectly *unintelligible*" (my italics).[8]

Using terminology introduced earlier, Berkeley's argument is an example of conceptual skepticism. He is not saying that we could never *know* that there are things (i.e., perceptions) existing independently of the mind; he is arguing that such an opinion is conceptually incoherent. Throughout this work I have argued that Hume resists such conceptually skeptical arguments for they stand in the way of his general program of describing our everyday beliefs and explaining their causal origins. The present text provides yet another example of this pattern of reasoning, for he tries to avoid what at first sight seems to be a "palpable contradiction." Here is what he says:

> we may observe, that what we call a *mind*, is nothing but a heap or collection of different perceptions, united together by certain relations, and supposed, tho' falsely, to be endow'd with a perfect simplicity and identity. Now as every perception is distinguishable from another, and may be consider'd as separately existent; it evidently follows, that there is no absurdity in separating any particular perception from the mind; that is, in breaking off all its relations, with that connected mass of perceptions, which constitute a thinking being. (p. 207)

This is Hume's response to the supposed contradiction which, echoing Berkeley, he presents to himself. But the argument itself is a muddle. For the moment let us accept the claim that the mind "is nothing but a heap or collection of perceptions." We can also assume that Hume is right in saying that there is no contradiction in supposing that a perception that does stand in certain relations with the "connected mass of perceptions, which constitute a think-

Skepticism with Regard to the Senses

ing being" may not stand in such a relationship. Take the relation of coexistence: a perception that does coexist with all the rest might not have coexisted with them at all. For example, the collection of perceptions ABCDE could have existed missing only E, or conversely, E could have existed all by itself. But this independence from the particular items that do in fact make up the mind is not the kind of independence we are looking for. It does not show that E could have existed independently of any mind *simpliciter*. Here, Hume's argument seems to be an *ignoratio elenchi*.

There are other reasons to doubt that Hume can escape from Berkeleyan conceptual skepticism. In his attacks upon the philosophical theories that posit perceptions and objects as distinct entities, he often seems to traffic in Berkeleyan arguments. More carefully, he often employs arguments whose natural generalization yields precisely those used by the Bishop of Cloyne. Earlier Hume argued that the senses could give us no idea of a continued existence of their objects: "For that is a contradiction in terms, and supposes that the senses continue to operate, even after they have ceas'd all manner of operation" (p. 188). By a parity of reasoning we should also say that the objects of imagination are given to us only when the imagination continues to operate. The same can be said for the objects of memory or any other faculty we might consider. Philonous leads Hylas down this path in Berkeley's *First Dialogue*:

> *Hyl.* . . . What [is] more easy than to conceive a tree or house existing by itself, independent of, and unperceived by, any mind whatsoever? I do at this present time conceive them existing after that manner.
> *Phil.* How say you, Hylas, can you see a thing which is at the same time unseen?
> *Hyl.* No, that were a contradiction.
> *Phil.* It is not as great a contradiction to talk of *conceiving* a thing which is *unconceived*?
> *Hyl.* It is.
> *Phil.* The tree or house, therefore, which you think of is conceived by you?
> *Hyl.* How should it be otherwise?
> *Phil.* And what is conceived is surely in the mind?

Hyl. Without question, that which is conceived is in the mind.
. . .
Phil. You ackowledge then that you cannot possibly conceive, how any one corporeal thing should exist otherwise than in a mind?
Hyl. I do.
Phil. And yet you will earnestly contend for the truth of that which you cannot so much as conceive?[9]

Hume, of course, is no Hylas, for he considers false what Hylas concedes to be true. But this does not change the situation.

To be clear, I am not suggesting that Hume actually accepts Berkeley's argument: on the contrary, he is anxious to reject it. The difficulty is to find any systematic reason for his doing so. Hylas plainly goes wrong in acknowledging that "that which is conceived is in the mind," but Hume can hardly disagree on this point. A disagreement here would lead him to give up the thesis that that which is *perceived* (i.e., a perception) is in the mind. Though a salutary result in itself, this amounts to abandoning the entire empiricist framework within which the *Treatise* is written. It seems then that the *Treatise* contains enough Berkeleyan elements to make the march to a conceptual skepticism concerning unperceived entities inevitable, and the argument he interposes to block this development is merely desperate. A little bit of Berkeley is always too much.

However any of this may be, Hume still thinks that he has responded to the threat that his position will collapse into Berkeley's, and he is thus able to hold that the belief in a continued and distinct existence of perceptions, though false, is still conceivable. This allows him to go forward to explain how we come to reside belief in this palpable falsehood. He simply invents a new version of his theory of vivacity transfer:

> we have a propensity to feign the continu'd existence of all sensible objects; and as this propensity arises from some lively impressions of the memory, it bestows a vivacity on that fiction; or in other words, makes us believe the continu'd existence of body. (p. 209)

Once more we have the standard pattern: (i) an argument showing that a belief has no rational foundation, (ii) an attempt to avoid

Skepticism with Regard to the Senses

conceptual skepticism so that the object of belief is not compromised, and (iii) a naturalistic account of the origin of that belief. I need only add that Hume once more avoids prescriptive skepticism:

> [I] take it for granted, whatever may be the reader's opinion at this present moment, that an hour hence he will be persuaded there is both an external and internal world. (p. 218)

Or as Hume said at the very beginning of his discussion of our belief in the existence of body:

> Nature has not left this to [our] choice, and has doubtless esteem'd it an affair of too great importance to be trusted to our uncertain reasonings and speculations. (p. 187)

Why this false belief should be esteemed of great importance is not explained.

VII

HUME'S NATURAL HISTORY OF PHILOSOPHY

The thought that ideas have a history, i.e., that they arise in a primitive form, then undergo systematic development, is usually associated with nineteenth-century philosophy. Of course, earlier philosophers were concerned with the source or origin of ideas, but the notion that ideas emerge systematically out of other ideas, for example out of tensions between conflicting ideas, is usually associated with such philosophers as Hegel and Marx. Yet this doctrine has an important place in Hume's philosophy, a fact, I think, that is not generally appreciated. In his *Natural History of Religion*, Hume tries to lay bare the principles that explain why religion begins with polytheism and then transforms itself into a monotheism. The work does not provide a profound insight into the nature of religious experience, but the thought that religion can be the subject of a *natural* history was a daring, and certainly heterodox, innovation. I shall argue that the developments in Part IV of Book I of the *Treatise* show precisely the same approach to the history of philosophy: philosophical positions arise and undergo transformations from natural causes that can be made intelligible by citing the operations of the human mind.[1]

The theme first emerges at the close of Hume's discussion of the causes that lead the plain man to (falsely) attribute continued and distinct existence to his private perceptions. Having completed this discussion, he turns to what he calls the philosophical view of these matters. After poking his eye and so on, the philosopher soon departs from the plain man's opinion that what he is aware of (i.e., his own perceptions) has a continued and distinct existence. In response to this, the philosopher adopts a theory of *double existence*, that is, he distinguishes between

> perceptions and objects, of which the former are suppos'd to be interrupted, and perishing, and different at every different return; the latter to be uninterrupted, and to preserve a continu'd existence and identity. (p. 211)

Hume says two things about this view: (i) "there are no principles either of the understanding or fancy, which lead us directly to embrace this opinion of the double existence of perceptions and objects," and (ii) "nor can we arrive at it but by passing thro' the common hypothesis of the identity and continuance of our interrupted perceptions" (p. 211).

Hume's first thesis, which we shall examine in a moment, moves along standard lines. He will first argue that this philosophical view is incapable of reasonable defense. He argues next, or perhaps just states, that it has no *primary* foundation in the imagination either. But despite all this, it remains a fact that philosophers have accepted this position however unfounded and, indeed, absurd, it might be. Hume saw that this too is a mental phenomenon in need of explanation. Explaining the origins and character of philosophical positions (including his own) forms an important part of Hume's Science of Man. Thus in Section II of Part IV, Hume discusses the philosopher's view of double existence; in Section III he examines the "fictions of the antient philosophy, concerning *substances*, and *substantial forms*, and *accidents*, and *occult qualities*" (p. 219); and then in Section IV he examines modern philosophy's distinction between primary and secondary qualities. In each case Hume not only rejects these positions, but attempts to provide an account of why philosophers have produced them and given them their assent.

Double Existence. It takes only a paragraph for Hume to argue that the double existence theory is not grounded in the principles of reason and understanding. Hume goes directly to the question whether this doctrine could be derived from causal reasoning, for no plausibility resides in the other possibilities: the doctrine of double existence cannot be an intuitive or demonstrative truth, nor can it be a matter of immediate experience. So the philosopher's theory of double existence can have its foundation only in causal reasoning, but that, Hume argues, is not possible either, as no beings are ever present to the mind but perceptions; it follows that we may observe a conjunction or a relation of cause and effect between different perceptions, but can never observe it between perceptions and objects. 'Tis impossible, therefore, that from the existence or any of the qualities of the former, we can ever form any conclusion concerning the existence of the latter, or ever satisfy our reason in this particular. (p. 212)

So far we have moved along familiar lines and we might expect that Hume will now make his standard move of attributing the origin of an idea together with causes of our assenting to it to the principles of the imagination. This, in fact, is what he does, but he first interpolates an argument to the effect that the theory of double existence has no *primary* recommendation to the imagination (p. 212). Hume puts his argument in the form of a challenge:

Let it be taken for granted, that our perceptions are broken, and interrupted, and however like, are still different from each other; and let any one upon this supposition shew why the fancy, directly and immediately, proceeds to the belief of another existence, resembling these perceptions in their nature, but yet continu'd, and uninterrupted, and identical. (pp. 212–13)

From this starting point, the natural (though false) view that recommends itself to the fancy is that our perceptions themselves have a continued and distinct existence. Hume has already tried to explain the mechanisms by which this takes place. Hume simply challenges the double-existence theorists to give a similar explanation of their position starting from the same place.

Hume's own suggestion is that the philosopher's doctrine of double existence is a *secondary* product of the imagination. It arises in the following way: The philosopher, like anyone else, has a strong propensity to believe in the continued existence of what he perceives. But after reflection, he comes to see that our perceptions are dependent and can have no continued and distinct existence. Here, as a reflective person, he should embrace this new view and reject the opinion of the vulgar – even if he recognizes that he will be overborne by the vulgar opinion when he leaves his study. Instead, both views, though incompatible, continue to have influence, with the result that a philosophical fiction is added to the fiction of the vulgar:

> The imagination tells us, that our resembling perceptions have a continu'd and uninterrupted existence, and are not annihilated by their absence. Reflection tells us, that even our resembling perceptions are interrupted in their existence, and different from each other. The contradiction betwixt these opinions we elude by a new fiction, which is conformable to the hypotheses both of reflection and fancy, by ascribing these contrary qualities to different existences; the *interruption* to perceptions, and the *continuance* to objects. (p. 215)

In this context – as in so many others – Hume invokes an image of opposing forces:

> But tho' our natural and obvious principles here prevail above our study'd reflections, 'tis certain there must be some struggle and opposition in the case; at least so long as these reflections retain any force of vivacity. (pp. 214–15)

The mind then moves to resolve this conflict: "In order to set ourselves at ease in this particular, we contrive a new hypothesis, which seems to comprehend both these principles of reason and imagination" (p. 215). Here the word "contrive" suggests a self-conscious effort to find some idea that will satisfy these two inconsistent demands. I don't think that this is what Hume intends, for, among other things, this would not explain the philosopher's tendency to believe his theory. The theory of double existence is not a mere artifice – it is a doctrine that naturally arises when we are under the double influence of the vulgar view of the continued and distinct existence of perceptions and the philosophical view that is incompatible with this.

Of the Antient Philosophy. This section continues Hume's naturalistic explanation of the emergence of philosophical positions. It begins with a conceit: Hume compares the ancient philosophical systems with dreams. But Hume does not view dreams as a system of almost impenetrable symbols; instead, dreams are taken to be transparent indicators of character, for in dreams "artifice, fear, and policy have no place, and men can neither be hypocrites with themselves nor others" (p. 219). Then, rather condescendingly, he remarks:

> In like manner, I am persuaded, there might be several useful discoveries made from a criticism of the fictions of the antient philosophy, concerning *substances, and substantial forms, and accidents, and occult qualities*; which, however unreasonable and capricious, have a very intimate connexion with the principles of human nature. (p. 219)

That philosophical fictions have their source in the principles of the human mind follows simply from Hume's naturalistic approach to belief; that these caprices have "intimate connexion with the principles of human nature" is a remarkable extension of this naturalistic approach.

On Hume's theory – which he attributes to the "most judicious philosophers" – "our ideas of bodies are nothing but collections form'd by the mind of the ideas of the several distinct sensible qualities, of which objects are compos'd, and which we find to have a constant union with each other" (p. 219). This, I think, is a phenomenalist point: when we view the object as a collection of perceptions (which, for Hume, it really is) then this separateness and looseness become evident to us. Seeing the world in this way is primitive to Hume's philosophy. All the same, in common life we view this compound "as ONE thing, and as continuing the SAME under very considerable alterations" (p. 219). That is, we falsely attribute *simplicity* (at a time) and *identity* (over time) to this bundle of discrete and changing perceptions. Here Hume speaks of a *contradiction* between two aspects of the human mind: the object given to us in sense is evidently composed of discrete parts which are discontinuous over time, yet we believe that this collection of discrete parts possesses a unity and simplicity that persists through time. These contradictory tendencies stand in need of explanation:

> It may, therefore, be worth while to consider the *causes*, which make us almost universally fall into such evident contradictions, as well as the *means* by which we endeavour to conceal them. (p. 219)

Hume's causal account of this phenomenon has the following form: given an unchanging series of perceptions, there is an easy transition from one idea to another which, Hume says, is the "essence" of the relation of *identity* (p. 220). In a given sequence, there may be changes that at each stage are relatively small so that the transitions will be smooth, and this leads to a standard associationist explanation:

> The smooth and uninterrupted progress of the thought, being alike in both cases, readily deceives the mind, and makes us ascribe an identity to the changeable succession of connected qualities. (p. 220)

A similar account is given for our mistaken belief in the simplicity of complex objects. Where the co-existent parts of a body are connected together "by a strong relation," they strike the mind in much the same manner in which a simple object strikes it. Once more an association leads us to identify similar phenomena, and the closely related complex is taken to be simple.

Although these errors are natural, the human mind sometimes has difficulties disguising them from itself. This occurs in rather different ways with respect to identity and simplicity. For *identity* the error becomes apparent from within the commonsense standpoint itself. With *simplicity*, the error is only seen when we adopt a philosophical standpoint. Taking identity first, as Hume does, the small changes over time may pass unnoticed, but if we view an object at two distant points in time, we cannot fail to recognize the change: "the variations, which were insensible when they arose gradually, do now appear of consequence, and seem entirely to destroy the identity" (p. 220). The conflict thus arises when the mind compares its objects from two different perspectives:

(i) When the object is viewed continuously through a series of relatively small changes, the transition is easy and we believe that we are dealing with the self-same thing enduring over time.

(ii) When the object is viewed from two separate points of view after a considerable change has taken place, the transition from one idea to the other is not easy and the notion of identity is destroyed.

It is at this point that the fiction of substance presents itself:

> In order to reconcile which contradictions the imagination is apt to feign something unknown and invisible, which it

supposes to continue the same under all these variations; and this unintelligible something it calls a *substance, or original and first matter.* (p. 220)

The method of dealing with simplicity is broadly similar, but there is an important difference worth examining. Hume begins by noting that when the parts of an object are closely related, the "fancy feels not the transition in passing from one part to another," and therefore, the compound object is felt to be a single thing. Now if the reasoning here followed the pattern of the discussion for identity, we might expect Hume to argue that this illusion is broken when we consider two quite disconnected parts of the object. What he says instead is more interesting:

> But the mind rests not here. Whenever it views the object in another light, it finds that all these qualities are different, and distinguishable, and separable from each other; which view of things being destructive of its primary and more natural notions, obliges the imagination to feign an unknown something, or *original* substance and matter, as a principle of union or cohesion among these qualities. (p. 221)

Exactly what does Hume have in mind by this notion of *viewing the object in another light*? Furthermore, why should this viewpoint be less primary and less natural? After all, what Hume calls the primary and more natural view is just the idea that the object is a simple whole, and, again, that idea is false.

I think that there are two ways in which we might understand this second viewpoint. Perhaps Hume is thinking about the causal reasoning that has led philosophers to recognize that we are aware only of perceptions and that these perceptions cannot have a continued and distinct existence. If this is the correct account, which I doubt, then this discussion parallels the earlier discussion of double existence, where a philosophical view and a common view came into conflict and this conflict was speciously resolved by a philosophical fiction. I think, however, that another reading fits the exact wording of the text better. Here Hume does not speak about reasoning of any kind, but about *viewing* the object, as he says, in *another light*. We can describe this new perspective on the object in various ways. For Hume, it is viewing the object as a perception (or as a collection of perceptions). We treat the

Hume's Natural History of Philosophy

object as something *given* to us. We immerse ourselves in the immediate appearance of the thing. We place it under a phenomenalist gaze. Hume's claim is that when we adopt this standpoint, the disconnectedness of the parts of the object becomes manifest to us.

In recent years we have learned to despise such talk about the *given*, *immediate experience*, etc. Yet it seems to me that there *is* a way of considering an object that inclines us to say, with Berkeley, that our perceptions are "visibly inert" or, with Kant, that "the manifold of experience will not synthesize itself." From this standpoint we are also inclined to say such things as this: "Only *I* am aware of this!" There is a way of viewing objects that inclines us toward solipsism.[2] Together these inclinations lead us to Hume's position that each individual is aware only of his own perceptions and these perceptions form a loose, unconnected bundle.

It is not easy to discuss this doctrine without being superficial. We may first notice that, for Hume, this standpoint – though not primary or natural – is *privileged*. From this standpoint we speak the truth, for the objects of experience are our own perceptions and they are separate and loose. The contrary opinions of common sense are more natural, in some way more primary, and apparently more important; yet they are false. Here various responses are possible. We might find this notion of viewing objects in *another way* completely unintelligible. (We might share O. K. Bouwsma's inability to follow G. E. Moore's instructions for picking out sense data – where Moore pointed to sense data, Bouwsma could find only knuckles, hair, and, at last, a rubber glove.[3]) With more sympathy we might agree that objects can be viewed in the way that Hume suggests, and we may even feel the inclination to say the things that he says when this viewpoint is adopted. But we can go this far and still deny that this perspective is *privileged*, that is, we can deny that this perspective and only this perspective is revelatory of how things really are. We can suggest instead that this dissociated viewpoint is artificial and dependent upon the common view of the world. Phenomenalist language is the strange language that emerges (naturally enough) when we view the world in a strange and artificial way. Finally, of course, we can agree with Hume that it is only when we depart from the common standpoint and view the world "in another light" that we apprehend things as they are.

Anyway, if we grant that it is possible to view the world in the way that Hume suggests, then once more a conflict emerges:

(i) From the common standpoint the objects about us seem to be single things whose parts form a united whole.
(ii) When viewed from a philosophical standpoint all the parts of the object seem entirely separate and loose.

To resolve this conflict, the imagination feigns "an unknown something, or *original* substance and matter, as a principle of union or cohesion among these qualities, and as what may give the compound object a title to be call'd one thing, notwithstanding its diversity and composition" (p. 221).

Looking back, we see that the recurrent theme in this discussion is that a conflict emerges within the mind and this conflict is speciously resolved by the production of the fiction. In each case, at least one party to the conflict is the common sense view of the world, but the other party varies in interesting ways. This becomes clear in the following summary of this discussion:

(i) The Philosopher's Theory of Double Existence.
This fiction emerges from a conflict between the *vulgar* view that what we perceive has a continued and distinct existence and the *philosophical* view that we are aware only of our own perceptions and these do not exist unperceived. The vulgar view is the product of the *imagination*; the philosophical view is the product of *causal* reasoning.
(ii) The Fiction of an Underlying Substance Enduring through Time.
This fiction emerges from a conflict within the common sense standpoint. When a thing passes through a series of small proportional changes, we tend to think that it remains the self-same thing despite these changes. When, however, we compare the thing at one time with the way it was at some distant time, we are struck by a large proportional change and our belief in the identity over time disappears. Here the conflict seems to be between imagination on the one hand and perceptions and memory on the other.

Hume's Natural History of Philosophy

(iii) The Fiction of an Underlying Substance that Unifies the Disparate Parts of an Object.
This fiction emerges from a conflict between the vulgar viewpoint where objects are apprehended as unified wholes and the philosophical viewpoint where they are recognized as mere congeries of distinct perceptions. Again, imagination is the source of the vulgar view whereas the philosophical view is a new, more immediate, way of viewing the world.

Notice that in each case, the philosophical view adds its own fiction to a fiction already present in the view of the vulgar.

The central idea of this discussion is that these various fictions arise naturally, usually masking interruptions or discontinuities in the flow of experience. This is the role of the immediate fictions of the plain man, but it is also the role of the secondary fictions that philosophy produces to replace the plain man's fictions that its sophistication has destroyed. Philosophical fictions are secondary in the sense that the prior existence of the plain man's fictions is a *causal* condition for their coming into existence. Both kinds of fiction are natural products of the imagination whose etiologies can be disclosed within the Science of Man.

Of Modern Philosophy – continues Hume's survey of philosophical positions. The broad thesis is that the conceits of our modern philosophy stand up to close scrutiny no better than the fictions of ancient philosophy. But the argument here is subtle, and in the end transcends its particular target – the distinction between primary and secondary qualities – to call into question the coherence of our faculties themselves. The discussion begins with Hume responding to a criticism that he poses for himself:

> But here it may be objected, that the imagination, according to my own confession, being the ultimate judge of all systems of philosophy, I am unjust in blaming the antient philosophers for making use of that faculty, and allowing themselves to be entirely guided by it in their reasonings. (p. 225)

In answering this criticism, Hume does not deny that on his system the imagination is the ultimate judge of all systems of philosophy. Its primacy here is but an instance of its central role in the formation of all beliefs beyond immediate experience. Instead, to defend himself, he draws a distinction between principles in the imagination

> which are permanent, irresistible, and universal; such as the customary transition from causes to effects, and from effects to causes: And the principles, which are changeable, weak, and irregular; such as those I have just now taken notice of. (p. 225)

Our belief in causes is an unavoidable and useful product of the imagination; the ancient belief in substance was neither. Our question, then, is this: does modern philosophy's acceptance of a distinction between primary and secondary qualities "arise only from the solid, permanent, and consistent principles of the imagination" (p. 226) or, like the fictions of ancient philosophy, does it arise from "principles, which, however common, are neither universal nor unavoidable in human nature" (p. 226)?

Hume's question is straightforward; his answer to it is not. Using the standard argument from variability of perceptions, Hume concludes that "many of our impressions [in particular, of colors, sounds, tastes, heat and cold] have no external model or archetype" (p. 227). For this reason, the double existence theorist (and the doctrine of primary qualities is a last ditch effort to save this theory) must exclude "sounds, colours, heat, cold, and other sensible qualities, from the rank of continu'd independent existences" (p. 227). We are thus left, he tells us, with "what are called primary qualities, as the only *real* ones" (p. 227) i.e., as the only qualities that we may properly attribute to the distinct external object.

In the *Principles*, Berkeley rejected this position because, among other things, he held that "extension, figure, and motion, abstracted from all other qualities, are inconceivable."[4] Hume says the same thing, arguing that it is impossible "to form an idea of this object or existence, without having recourse to the secondary and sensible qualities" (p. 230). Hume's only addition to Berkeley's argument is a detailed refutation of appeals to *solidity* to solve this problem. In any case, his basic conclusion is the same as Berkeley's: "Our modern philosophy, therefore, leaves us no just nor satisfactory idea of . . . matter" (p. 229).

Going back to the beginning of the discussion, we now see that our modern philosophy, with its distinction between primary and secondary qualities, is in the same boat as the ancient philosophy: they both deal in unintelligibilia. This is certainly part of what Hume wants to say, but it is not, I think, the whole story or even the most important part of it. Recall Hume's account of the source of the ancient philosopher's fictions: they arose from principles of the imagination, but not from principles that are "universal or unavoidable." What about the modern philosopher's doctrine of independent existents characterized solely by primary qualities? Of course, that doctrine isn't universal or unavoidable either; most humans have never heard of it. If, however, we turn our attention to the mechanism in the imagination that leads the philosopher to adopt such a position, we make a startling discovery. The doctrine of primary qualities arises from a conflict between two regular products of the imagination. First, we are all naturally and inevitably led to believe in the continued and distinct existence of much that we perceive. This is a belief of common life, not a philosopher's fiction. The philosopher creates the fiction of an independent existence, as we have seen, in order to preserve some part of the plain man's view which the experimental method has shown to be false. But these same experimental methods also show that many of the features of our perceptions cannot characterize this external object. Paring away these features, we are left with an independent existent that possesses only primary qualities. It is important to see that this part of the argument also appeals to the regular principles of the imagination. Hume tells us that the conclusions drawn from the argument for perceptual variability are "as satisfactory as can possibly be imagined" (p. 227). Yet the upshot of these two regular operations of the imagination is a doctrine that is incomprehensible. Thus the imagination, even when behaving properly, can lead us into the abyss of skepticism. Hume puts it this way:

> Thus there is a direct and total opposition betwixt our reason and our senses; or more properly speaking, betwixt those conclusions we form from cause and effect, and those that persuade us of the continu'd and independent existence of body. When we reason from cause and effect, we conclude, that neither colour, sound, taste, nor smell have a continu'd and independent existence. When we exclude these sensible

qualities there remains nothing in the universe, which has such an existence. (p. 231)

In the *Enquiry*, as we noted earlier, Hume drew a distinction between a species of skepticism that is "antecedent to all study and philosophy" and a skepticism that is "consequent to science and inquiry." Hume there dismisses antecedent skepticism, which he associates with Descartes, as a game that we are unable to play – and unable to win, if we could play. Consequent skepticism, on the other hand, is a persistent feature of the Humean landscape. When we lay bare the mechanisms that generate our ideas and induce our assent to them, they seem to have no legitimate title to do so. The causes of belief, however effective when they operate unnoticed, do not translate into reasons for belief when subjected to critical inquiry. The opposite is true: the further we carry our inquiries into the mechanisms of belief formation, the more skeptical we become. Hume put it this way:

> 'Tis impossible upon any system to defend either our understanding or senses; and we but expose them farther when we endeavour to justify them in that manner. As the sceptical doubt arises naturally from a profound and intense reflection on those subjects, it always encreases, the farther we carry our reflections, whether in opposition or conformity to it. (p. 218)

Skepticism, especially Pyrrhonian skepticism, is not a stable position. When we enter into the affairs of daily life, at most we will maintain a moderate or mitigated skepticism of the kind that Hume applauds. Yet Pyrrhonism is the natural outcome of philosophical reflection. It is also the final outcome of intense reflection, for we do not overcome it by reflecting still more deeply, but by bringing our reflections to an end.

VIII

THE SOUL AND THE SELF

Section VI of Part IV contains Hume's famous discussion of personal identity. This section has attracted attention because Hume himself expressed his dissatisfaction with it, saying, in an Appendix to the *Treatise*, "I neither know how to correct my former opinions, nor how to render them consistent" (p. 633). He presents his difficulties in these words:

> In short there are two principles, which I cannot render consistent; nor is it in my power to renounce either of them, viz. *that all our distinct perceptions are distinct existences*, and *that the mind never perceives any real connexion among distinct existences*. (p. 636)

At the very least, this passage demands a charitable reading, for the principles cited are not inconsistent with one another. Presumably, these two principles taken together are inconsistent with some third principle that Hume also finds himself incapable of abandoning and that principle must somehow concern personal identity. Yet Hume never says explicitly what is bothering him, and no consensus has emerged among commentators concerning what it might be.[1] Now Hume's discussion of personal identity is preceded by a section concerning the immateriality of the soul. This earlier discussion provides much of the framework for this latter more famous part of the *Treatise*, and, indeed, it may, as I shall argue, be the source of Hume's concerns about the consistency of his system. The section is interesting in another way as well: in declaring that "the question concerning the substance of

The Soul and the Self

the soul is absolutely unintelligible" (p. 250), Hume seems to embrace a conceptual skepticism which, as I have argued, is uncharacteristic of the *Treatise*.

Though the discussion will take a number of surprising twists and turns, the section entitled "Of the Immateriality of the Soul" opens straightforwardly by attacking the idea that the soul is an immaterial substance, where it is the soul's substantiality, not its immateriality, that is at issue. Hume asks those philosophers who debate whether the soul is a material or immaterial substance to tell us first, "*What they mean by substance and inhesion*? And after they have answer'd this question, 'twill then be reasonable, and not till then, to enter seriously into the dispute" (p. 232). Hume remarks that this question proved impossible to answer for matter and body, and then suggests, in an obscure passage, that an account of mental substance is burdened with special difficulties of its own:

> As every idea is deriv'd from a precedent impression, had we any idea of the substance of our minds, we must also have an impression of it; which is very difficult, if not impossible, to be conceiv'd. For how can an impression represent a substance, otherwise than by resembling it? And how can an impression resemble a substance, since, according to this philosophy, it is not a substance, and has none of the peculiar qualities or characteristics of a substance? (pp. 232-3)

Hume has in mind a philosopher who maintains that substance itself must be utterly different from any of its qualities, modes, or acts. If impressions are then taken to be qualities, modes, or acts of substance, then they cannot resemble substance and, given Hume's theory of the origin of ideas, we could have no idea (not even a fictitious idea) of substance.

After this dialectical flourish, Hume returns to his normal ways by asking what impression gives rise to the idea of the substance of our minds. His claim is that no such impression or idea can be found – a point he makes by asking a series of questions:

> Is it an impression of sensation or of reflection? Is it pleasant, or painful, or indifferent? Does it attend us at all times, or does it only return at intervals? If at intervals, at what times

principally does it return, and by what causes is it produc'd? (p. 233)

Hume completes his critique of the idea of a mental substance by rejecting a definitional trick. If substance is defined as "something which may exist by itself," then every impression or idea will itself be a substance, for every impression and idea is itself a distinct existence. In that case, it will make no sense to say that impressions actually *inhere* in the substance of the mind, since one substance cannot inhere in another. "Thus neither by considering the first origin of ideas, nor by means of a definition are we able to arrive at any satisfactory notion of substance" (p. 234).

With the main argument in hand, Hume turns to the supposed *simplicity* of the soul. He considers a proposed refutation of materialist conceptions of the soul that runs as follows. If the soul is an extended thing, then it will have parts, a top and a bottom, a left side and a right side, etc. From this it follows that any ideas that inhere in such a substance must themselves have a definite spatial location. Yet, according to Hume, "an object may exist, and yet be no where" (p. 235). For example:

> A moral reflection cannot be plac'd on the right or on the left hand of a passion, nor can a smell or sound be either of a circular or a square figure. These objects and perceptions, so far from requiring any particular place, are absolutely incompatible with it, and even the imagination cannot attribute it to them. (p. 236)

From this it follows that there are perceptions which are "incapable of any conjunction in place with matter or body" (p. 236).[2]

Having condemned the materialists, "who conjoin all thought with extension" (p. 239), Hume is quick to point out that a like argument will embarrass their opponents, "who conjoin all thought with a simple and indivisible substance" (p. 239). The reason for this is that some of our ideas are extended:

> to cut short all disputes, the very idea of extension is copy'd from nothing but an impression, and consequently must perfectly agree to it. To say the idea of extension agrees to any thing, is to say it is extended. (pp. 239–40)

Now the immaterialist must labor under the same difficulties that

The Soul and the Self

confounded the materialist: he must explain how something extensionless can be locally conjoined with something extended:

> Is the indivisible subject, or immaterial substance, if you will, on the left or on the right hand of the perception? Is it in this particular part, or in that other? Is it in every part without being extended? (p. 240)

So we arrive at a perfect symmetry in the difficulties with both the theory that the subject is a material substance and the theory that the subject is an immaterial substance. Neither theory can explain the local conjunction of the extended with the unextended. Yet it seems that the soul, if it is a substance, must be either a material substance or an immaterial substance. Since both views lead to the same absurdities, we seem forced to abandon the substantial theory of the soul altogether.

> To pronounce, then, the final decision upon the whole; the question concerning the substance of the soul is *absolutely unintelligible*: All our *perceptions* are not susceptible of a local union, either with what is extended or unextended; there being some of them of the one kind, and some of the other. (p. 250) (The italics are mine. I shall return to this passage later.)

The section on the immateriality of the soul contains a third, and very important, argument: Hume clears materialism of the charge that it is absurd in suggesting that matter in motion can give rise to thought. On Hume's account of causality, causal relationships between material and immaterial objects are no more (or less) mysterious than causal relationships between material objects or causal relationships between immaterial objects.

> Now as all objects, which are not contrary, are susceptible of a constant conjunction, and as no real objects are contrary; it follows, that for ought we can determine by the mere ideas, any thing may be the cause or effect of any thing. (pp. 249–50)[3]

This is Hume's solution to one of the central problems of modern philosophy: the so-called mind-body interaction problem. If Hume's theory of causation is correct, this solution is, of course, perfectly adequate.

The Soul and the Self

There are then three central theses in this section of the *Treatise:* (i) both the materialist and the immaterialist face insuperable problems explaining the local union of objects that are extended with those that are not extended; (ii) "the question concerning the substance of the soul is absolutely unintelligible"; and (iii) if causality can be correctly defined in terms of constant conjunction, then "matter and motion may often be regarded as the causes of thought." But even if this correctly summarizes the content of this section, it does not capture its main rhetorical force. As the title indicates, Hume is primarily interested in the doctrine of the immateriality of the soul and, more specifically, with the notion of *simplicity* that is associated with it. This emphasis comes out in a variety of ways. Most interestingly, after completing a largely even-handed critique of both the materialist and immaterialist doctrines of a substantial self, Hume interpolates an additional six pages of criticism aimed specifically at the "doctrine of the immateriality, simplicity, and indivisibility of a thinking substance" (p. 240). Hume, in one of his few lapses into an assertion of guilt by association, claims that anyone who holds that the mind is simple and indivisible must also accept Spinoza's "atheist" doctrine of "the simplicity of the universe, and the unity of that substance, in which he supposes both thought and matter to inhere" (p. 240). He doesn't say why.[4]

Finally, in the closing paragraph of Section V, Hume offers an "apology" that reveals the source of his interest in the simplicity of the mind. He assures the reader that his arguments are in no way dangerous to religion. Such assurances are needed because his denial of the simplicity of the mind seems to deprive religion of one of its standard proofs of the immortality of the soul. Hume's ingenious reply is that his arguments have no such tendency since proofs of the immortality of the soul based upon its supposed simplicity are no good anyway.

> Any object may be imagin'd to become entirely inactive, or to be annihilated in a moment; and 'tis an evident principle, *that whatever we can imagine, is possible.* Now this is no more true of matter, than of spirit; of an extended compounded substance, than of a simple and unextended. In both cases the metaphysical arguments for the immortality of the soul are equally inconclusive. (p. 250)

The Soul and the Self

Hume then gives the discussion a wonderful turn by continuing in these words: "and in both cases the moral arguments and those deriv'd from the analogy of nature are equally strong and convincing" (p. 250). That, of course, does not mean there *are* strong moral and analogical proofs for the immortality of an immaterial soul, and, in fact, the plain implication is just the reverse. Defenders of religion would reject proofs for the immortality of a material soul and thus will not be happy to learn that their proofs for the immortality of an immaterial soul are exactly on a par with them. Hume caps this discussion with a sentence that could have been written by Montaigne:

> If my philosophy, therefore, makes no addition to the arguments for religion, I have at least the satisfaction to think it takes nothing from them, but that every thing remains precisely as before. (pp. 250–1)

I think we can now understand why Hume spends so much time discussing the simplicity of the soul: it provides an occasion for some mischievous fun at the expense of doctrines of divinity and school metaphysics.

But Hume's discussion of the *simplicity* does not end with Section V of Part IV; it continues into Section VI where the supposed simplicity of the *self* at a time is examined in tandem with its supposed identity over time. In a famous passage he tells us:

> The mind is a kind of theatre, where several perceptions successively make their appearance; pass, re-pass, glide away, and mingle in an infinite variety of postures and situations. There is properly no *simplicity* in it at one time, nor *identity* in different; whatever natural propension we may have to imagine that simplicity and identity. (p. 253)

Hume then goes on at length to explain the origins of "so great a propension to ascribe an identity of these successive perceptions, and to suppose ourselves possest of an invariable and uninterrupted existence thro' the whole course of our lives" (p. 253). This, of course, concerns the *identity* of the self over time and it is only at the end of his discussion that Hume again considers the *simplicity* of the self, remarking that the account he has given of

The Soul and the Self

identity "may be extended with little or no variation to that of *simplicity*" (p. 263).

In general, the discussion proceeds along the same lines that we found earlier in the section on ancient philosophy, where Hume invoked the associationist principles of resemblance and causality to explain the plain man's (false) belief in the identity of material objects or bodies over time. There is, however, one feature of this discussion that merits digression. At one point Hume makes the following, somewhat obscure, remark:

> Thus the controversy concerning identity is not merely a dispute of words. For when we attribute identity, in an improper sense, to variable or interrupted objects, our mistake is not confin'd to the expression, but is commonly attended with a fiction, either of something invariable and uninterrupted, or of something mysterious and inexplicable, or at least with a propensity to such fictions. (p. 255)

We might think that Hume would argue that debates over personal identity *are* merely verbal just because personal identity is a fiction, but, in fact, he says just the opposite. Later he makes essentially the same point with more clarity:

> as the relations, and the easiness of the transition may diminish by insensible degrees, we have no just standard, by which we can decide any dispute concerning the time, when they acquire or lose a title to the name of identity. All the disputes concerning the identity of connected objects are merely verbal, except so far as the relation of parts gives rise to some fiction or imaginary principle of union, as we have already observ'd. (p. 262)

The first sentence makes clear which disputes concerning identity *are* merely verbal: disputes that concern where to draw the line between the preservation and loss of identity through a series of changes. As he says, we have no *just standard* to answer this question. This same notion appears in an exchange that occurs in Part XII of the *Dialogues Concerning Natural Religion*. Philo is speaking:

> there is a species of controversy, which, from the very nature of language and of human ideas, is involved in perpetual

The Soul and the Self

ambiguity, and can never, by any precaution or any definitions, be able to reach a reasonable certainty or precision. These are the controversies concerning the degrees of any quality or circumstance.[5]

So if a dispute broke out among the vulgar as to whether a given person was still the same person after some considerable change, then that dispute would be both verbal and incurable. The situation is quite different for the philosophical dispute concerning the existence of a substantial self that endures through changes. Such a substantial self does not exist. It is a fiction. It is a fiction invented – though presumably not self-consciously – by philosophers to lend respectability to the belief they share with the vulgar concerning personal identity. The philosophical dispute is not verbal and incurable, for we can say that the doctrine that the mind is simple at one time and identical over time is just false.

Returning to the main line of reasoning in the text, Hume seems to be writing with perfect self-confidence. The discussion of the simplicity and identity of the self parallels the earlier discussion of the simplicity and identity of material objects. There may be differences in emphasis between the earlier discussion of material substance and the present discussion of the self. The earlier discussion dwells rather longer on the concept of identity, whereas this latter discussion gives more emphasis to the associative mechanisms that bring about a belief in identity. On the whole, however, the two discussions are very similar and show Hume developing characteristic features of his philosophy with perfect confidence. Why then, in the Appendix to the *Treatise*, does Hume declare himself unable to render his system consistent? Precisely what inconsistency does he have in mind; and why does he find it intractable?

I do not think that I can give a fully satisfactory answer to these questions, for the text, as far as I can see, is underdetermined on these matters. Furthermore, it is all too easy to mix up our opinions about what Hume *ought* to have been worried about with what, in fact, he was worried about. For example, throughout the *Treatise*, Hume adopts two different images of the mind or self. The first, and official, view is that the mind is a bundle (heap, collection) of perceptions. The second view adopts the metaphor of a theatre where the mind appears as a spectator to the scenes

The Soul and the Self

presented to it. "The mind is a kind of theatre, where several perceptions successively make their appearance" (p. 253). In this context Hume immediately appends a warning: "The comparison of the theatre must not mislead us. They are the successive perceptions only, that constitute the mind" (p. 253). Well and good, but spectatorial imagery occurs throughout the *Treatise* and often seems essential for the intelligibility of Hume's argument. So it might seem, especially to one who looks back at the *Treatise* from a Kantian perspective, that Hume finally recognized the need for a unified conscious self and then despaired of supplying it given his own principles. I think that it may be right that Hume ought to have recognized the need for a *transcendental* judging self and it is surely right that his own principles could not have supplied this need, yet I see no evidence in the text that his worries took this form. Indeed, there is one place in the text, the passage just cited, where he specifically warns against taking his spectatorial images literally.

Another more plausible suggestion is that Hume needs a genuinely enduring *empirical* self to underlay the associative mechanisms that form the core of his theory. Jane L. McIntyre formulates this interpretation of Hume's problem in these words: "the concept of a self that is *affected by experience* and therefore must *persist through experience* is precisely the concept of the self that *cannot* be accounted for in the context of the theory of ideas presented in the *Treatise*."[6] With variations in detail, this is the view of Hume's problem that has been presented by MacNabb, Passmore, Robison, and others.[7] Hume has no qualms about treating fundamental ideas as fictions, but it seems that his own theories demand a self that genuinely, and not just seemingly, endures over time. If Hume saw this point and conceded it, then we could understand the despair he expresses about the consistency of his system in the Appendix we are considering. But again I have yet to see any plausible citation of text indicating that Hume's worries actually took this form.[8]

Thus far we have examined two suggestions concerning the source of Hume's anxieties about the consistency of his system: one concerns the need for a unified *judging* self, something like a Kantian transcendental ego; the other concerns the need for an enduring *empirical* self as the seat for associationist mechanisms. There is explicit text that goes against the first interpretation

The Soul and the Self

and no text, as far as I can see, that supports the second. Both interpretations have this in common: they suppose that the system of the *Treatise* demands a genuine self – not merely a fictitious self – and is inconsistent without it. Other interpreters of Hume locate his worries in a different place: Hume's problem is not that his position demands a real self as opposed to a fictitious self; instead he finds his account of the production of this fiction itself inconsistent.

The chief thing to be said on behalf of characterizing Hume's problem in this second way is that it squares quite well with some of Hume's own language:

> Most philosophers seem inclin'd to think, that personal identity *arises* from consciousness; and consciousness is nothing but a reflected thought or perception. The present philosophy, therefore, has so far a promising aspect. But all my hopes vanish, when I come to explain the principles, that unite our successive perceptions in our thought or consciousness. I cannot discover any theory, which gives me satisfaction on this head. (pp. 635–6)

Notice that this passage does not point to any particular difficulty with the associationist accounts of the simplicity and identity of the self given in the main body of the text. There must, it seems, be some general reason why any such account will face profound difficulties, yet Hume, for all his self-critical candor, has not said exactly why these distinct ideas cannot have fictitious connections *via* the principles of association.

As already noted, Hume's account of the identity and simplicity of the self mimics his earlier account of the (fictitious) identity and simplicity of material objects. We can profitably ask why Hume is worried about the one and not the other, for, as David Pears shrewdly remarks, "He does not say anything that is not true of ordinary material objects, and his argument could equally well be applied to the identity of cabbages."[9] In both places he argues that a fiction is generated by the associative mechanisms founded on the relations of resemblance and of cause and effect. Is there anything special about the constituents of the mind that precludes such an associationist account of their membership in a mind that is unified both at a time and over time?

Various writers have noticed that it is not a *necessary* condition

The Soul and the Self

for membership in the bundle that a perception stand in a relationship of either resemblance or cause and effect to at least one other member of the bundle. Impressions of sensation illustrate this: an impression of sensation seems not to be *caused* by another perception and, since its content can be novel, it need not resemble any other perceptions either. Yet, for Hume, impressions of sensation are resident in the mind, indeed paradigmatically so. Stroud makes the point this way:

> What Hume needs is a causal chain that runs 'horizontally,' as it were, along the whole series of incoming perceptions that we get from moment to moment. That is what I am arguing does not exist. When I am having an impression of a tree I might turn my head and get an impression of a building, but the first impression is not a cause of the second.[10]

Although Stroud notes this difficulty, he does not argue that this is the source of Hume's anxieties expressed in the Appendix to the *Treatise*. Indeed, it would be very hard to make this case since there does not seem to be a shred of textual evidence indicating that Hume ever considered this particular difficulty.[11]

A second line of argument attacks the *sufficiency* of resemblance and causation to yield the idea of *my* self or of one particular self rather than another. In its simplest form, it can be maintained, as David Pears has maintained, that Hume's position is incapable of explaining the peculiarities of ownership of mental objects.[12] But this is not Hume's worry, nor does Pears suggest it is, for Hume explicitly says that there is nothing about a particular perception in itself that marks it as belonging to one bundle (e.g., the bundle that I am) rather than any other. Starting from this last point Stroud presents his interpretation of Hume's self-doubts:

> There is nothing in any perception, considered in itself, which implies the existence of any other perception, or of anything else whatsoever, and so there is nothing intrinsic to any perception that connects it with some particular series rather than another. So why do perceptions present themselves, so to speak, in discrete, separate bundles?[13]

The individuation of bundles is surely a problem for Hume, but where is the inconsistency Hume complains of? Perhaps discrete bundlehood is inexplicable as so many things are in Hume's philosophy. To this Stroud replies: "To say it is 'inexplicable' for Hume is to say that it is inconsistent with the theory of ideas which he takes to be the only way to make sense of psychological phenomena."[14] I don't find this persuasive, for Hume often admits that psychological phenomena are inexplicable (e.g., the operations of the imagination) without seeming to worry about the consistency of his position.

Garrett provides another ingenious variation on this theme by arguing as follows. Suppose there are two spatially non-locatable perceptions in the minds of A and B respectively. They might, for example, be passions. Furthermore, let us suppose that they occur simultaneously. How, on Hume's theory, are we to assign these two perceptions to different minds? Not by resemblance, for we have assumed that they are qualitatively identical. This leaves causality as the only possibility, but it doesn't seem to work either. Distinct causes can be separated only on the basis of spatial relations, which these perceptions lack, or temporal relations, which these two perceptions share. In sum, if A and B both simultaneously feel, say, the same deep sense of foreboding, there would be nothing in Hume's theory that would make sense of the fact that one of these feelings is A's, the other B's.[15]

I think this is a trenchant criticism and it is not immediately clear how Hume would answer it, but again we must ask where Garrett locates the inconsistency that Hume complains of. According to Garrett, Hume surely accepts the following proposition: "It is possible that two qualitatively identical perceptions of any kind, including those that are 'no where,' would occur in different minds at the same time."[16] I have no doubt that, if put to him, Hume would accept this possibility, then, given the argument that Garrett has presented, he would be forced to admit that "either both of [these perceptions] will belong to a given bundle of perceptions or neither of them will."[17]

Again no text is cited to show that Hume was even remotely worried about the ingenious problem that Garrett has posed; more to the point, it does not seem to be something that Hume was likely to be worried about. Hume was uncritically wedded to the way of ideas. He thought that he had immediate access to his own ideas and he simply took it for granted that these ideas were *his*. He saw quite clearly that this position had skeptical consequences

The Soul and the Self

concerning what can be *known* beyond the realm of immediate perceptions and it was an important part of his program to develop these skeptical consequences. As far as I can see, however, there is no reason to suppose that Hume entertained the conceptual worries attributed to him by Stroud and Garrett. More strongly, I think that such conceptual problems were quite alien to the standpoint that Hume, along with most philosophers of the seventeenth and eighteenth centuries, uncritically adopted.[18]

Turning now to suggestions I find more persuasive, I think that any suitable account of Hume's worries about personal identity should meet two minimum standards: (i) there should be textual support showing that Hume was at least aware of the issues under consideration; (ii) the inconsistency or difficulty pointed to should concern principles of some importance to Hume himself. I shall consider three proposals that go at least some distance toward meeting these demands.

The first is taken from Terence Penelhum. He claims that

> Hume is forced by his mistaken analysis of our concept of identity to interpret all ascription of identity to changing things as a mistaken ascription, and to regard the relationships that occasion it as distractions which make us overlook the diversity of their successive stages. He accordingly considers our belief in the unity of the self to be a commitment to a fiction.[19]

According to Penelhum, "Hume's fundamental error is his assertion that the idea of identity is the idea of an object that persists without changing."[20]

To see how this conception of identity could lead Hume into immediate trouble, consider the case of a person ascribing identity over time to himself. He might say of himself "I am the person who won the Grand Prix." If Hume's account of identity is correct, then this person would be saying of himself that he had in no way changed since winning the Grand Prix. That, however, is just false, and he cannot but know that it is false. Of course, Hume is fond of attributing false beliefs to the mass of mankind and then proposing *fictions* behind which they can be hidden. In the present case, however, the falsehood of unchangingness is so palpable that it seems inconceivable that it could be concealed by a fiction. Thus, starting from his curious conception of identity, Hume is led to the paradoxical result that human beings univers-

The Soul and the Self

ally accept a belief that should strike them all as false. This, in turn, would lead him to feel uneasy about his account of our *belief* in personal identity. If Penelhum is right, he should have looked more deeply into the concept of identity that was the genuine source of his difficulties.

My second suggestion assumes, along with Stroud and Garrett, that Hume was worried about the *fiction* of self-identity, and, in particular, he finds inconsistent his account of how such a fiction could come into existence. If we return to the discussion of the simplicity of the soul, we can find one good reason why Hume might have worried about the coherence of his position in this regard. Hume there argued that both the materialists and the immaterialists will be embarrassed when asked to explain how extended perceptions and extensionless perceptions can be locally conjoined. Because of the inconceivability of this local conjunction, he drew the conclusion that "the question concerning the substance of the soul is absolutely unintelligible" (p. 250). Later Hume may have realized that the very same considerations cut against the intelligibility of the *wholeness* (including both the *simplicity* and *identity*) of the self. Invoking causal relations between the extended and the extensionless ideas will not relieve this difficulty, for it is the *intelligibility* of conjoining the extended with the extensionless that is at issue, and this is prior to any inquiry concerning the supposed source of this conjunction. If Hume saw that his arguments intended to show the unintelligibility of a *unified* substantial self would apply equally well against *any* notion of a unified self, then we can understand his despair at giving an adequate account of this fiction.

My third proposal is more like those of MacNabb, Passmore, Robison and others in suggesting that Hume's position demands a *genuine* self rather than a merely fictitious self and is inconsistent without one. My reasons for saying this are, however, wholly different from theirs. Perhaps it has been pointed out before, but very little has been made of the fact that the *initial* appearance of the doctrine that the mind is a heap or collection of perceptions is in the section on *scepticism with regard to the senses*. There, as we saw, it was invoked to help Hume out of a desperate situation. It seems that it is not only false (as Hume maintains) but actually self-contradictory (as Berkeley held) to assert that a perception

The Soul and the Self

can exist unperceived. We can look again at Hume's efforts to avoid this difficulty:

> we may observe, that what we call a *mind*, is nothing but a heap or collection of different perceptions, united together by certain relations, and suppos'd, tho' falsely, to be endowed with a perfect simplicity and identity. Now as every perception is distinguishable from another, and may be consider'd as separately existent; it evidently follows, that there is no absurdity in separating any particular perception from the mind; that is, in breaking off all its relations, with that connected mass of perceptions, which constitute a thinking being. (p. 207)

In the light of our recent discussions, this passage must appear curious indeed. It starts out by denying the "perfect simplicity and identity" of that "heap or collection of perceptions" which is the mind in order to make sense of the idea of a perception existing outside of the mind – i.e., outside of such a heap. The passage concludes by speaking about the "*connected mass* of perceptions, which constitute a thinking being." Now in the Appendix it is just this connectedness that Hume finds himself unable to explain, and this does lead Hume into profound difficulties. Hume's argument against Berkeley depends upon the notion of an *individual* mind from which a perception may be separated, but Hume provides no principle for individuating heaps of perceptions into minds. Strictly speaking, each perception is itself an individual substance and, again strictly speaking, a collection or heap of individual substances is not an individual substance. More remarkably, on Hume's principles, each perception is an individual *mind*, and a collection of minds is not itself a mind. Less strictly, for Hume, perceptions must be connected together loosely enough to allow separation, while at the same time they must be connected together closely enough to constitute a mind from which things can be separated. Hume's radical atomism guarantees the first result, but precludes the second. Without both features (separable perceptions and a unified mind), Hume's theory of perception no longer contains a response to Berkeley's claim that it is self-contradictory to suppose that a perception can exist unperceived.[21]

Of the three proposals concerning the source of Hume's worries

The Soul and the Self

about personal identity, I prefer the third, both for textual and systematic reasons. Textually, I think it significant that Hume's heap theory of the mind makes its first explicit appearance in the discussion of our belief in the distinct existence of what we perceive. The discussion is systematically important because, as he sees, his whole position is threatened with collapse. There is, however, a challenge that remains embarrassing: if Hume's worries took any of these forms, *why didn't he say so?* I don't know the answer to this and I can only say that this challenge embarrasses everyone who puts forward suggestions on this matter. After all, Hume's explicit statement of his problem is that he cannot render the principle *that all our distinct perceptions are distinct existences* consistent with the further principle *that the mind never perceives any real connexion among distinct existences.* This, taken at face value, is the least plausible interpretation of all.

IX

REASON AND THE PASSIONS

This examination of the interplay between skepticism and naturalism in Hume's philosophy has focused primarily on Book I of the *Treatise*. This is not surprising, since Book I contains a series of skeptical arguments which bring, in turn, the understanding, reason, and the senses under attack. Indeed, the prominence of skeptical arguments in the first book of the *Treatise*, together with their independent interest, can lead the reader to undervalue the naturalistic program that these arguments are intended to further.

The situation in Book II is more or less the reverse of that in Book I. Book II concerns the passions, and, since it has not generally been supposed that the passions are the product of reasoning, there is no need for skeptical arguments showing that this is not so. Thus Book II sets directly to work producing naturalistic accounts of the human passions without first engaging in skeptical ground-clearing. The discussion involves an elaborate application of the laws of association in order to give a causal account of the relationships among various ideas, feelings, emotions, passions, and so on. Some of this discussion is obscure, much of it tedious, and some of the central doctrines seem plainly wrong. For all that, Book II offers the most sustained example of Hume pursuing his naturalistic program. Here, better than anywhere else, we see what he had in mind when he spoke of introducing the experimental method of reasoning into moral subjects.[1]

But even if naturalistic themes dominate Book II, it still has its

Reason and the Passions

skeptical moment. Traditionally, reason, in a broad sense, has been assigned two roles: in its theoretical employment, it is supposed to yield knowledge or, at least, well-founded belief; in its practical employment, it is supposed to regulate our passions and in this way govern our conduct. In the face of the fashionable stoicism of his day, Hume denies that reason can perform this second task, just as he previously denied that it can perform the first. His position is captured in a famous aphorism – often quoted, though not always accurately and almost never with reference to the context: "Reason is, and ought only to be the slave of the passions, and can never pretend to any other office than to serve and obey them" (p. 415). Most of what follows is an attempt to elucidate both the "is" and the "ought" in this pronouncement.

Hume's defense of his departure from traditional wisdom falls into three parts: (1) He argues that reason alone can never be a motive to any action of the will and draws from this the further conclusion that it can never oppose a passion in the direction of the will. (2) He adds to this the consideration that reason cannot be opposed to the passions for, in the strict sense, a passion can be neither reasonable nor unreasonable. (3) He ends by suggesting that this traditional view that reason is capable of opposing and controlling the passions is the result of a tendency to confuse the passionless operations of reason with the operations of the calmer passions which they much resemble. Arguments (1) and (2) play an important, though unwholesome, role in Hume's discussion of morals in Book III.

(1) Hume's first argument is intended to show that reason alone can neither give rise to actions nor oppose the tendency of a passion to give rise to action. The fundamental move bears a superficial resemblance to that pattern of argument that has come to be known as Hume's Fork, but, in fact, the style of reasoning is essentially different from that found, say, in Hume's skeptical argument concerning induction in the *Enquiry*. Hume does, indeed, begin by reminding us that the operations of the human understanding can be divided into two parts:

> The understanding exerts itself after two different ways, as it judges from demonstration or probability; as it regards the abstract relations of our ideas, or those relations of objects, of which experience only gives us information. (p. 413)

Reason and the Passions

The standard next move for Hume is to argue that neither operation can establish the truth of some claim, e.g., that the future will resemble the past or (as in the *Enquiry*) that the external world exists. Here, however, the question does not concern the understanding's ability to establish some truth, but instead, it concerns the capacity of that faculty to raise or suppress some passion and thereby produce or prevent some action.[2]

Hume's first point is that abstract reasoning on relations of ideas can never alone be the cause of an action. He recognizes that abstract reasoning, for example, mathematical reasoning, can have a bearing upon action, as when an engineer uses calculations to guide his constructions, but he claims that these cases always presuppose some antecedently given *purpose*. It is this purpose that secures the connection between thought and action. Now reasoning involved in achieving some purpose is, Hume argues, causal in character, so we may now turn our attention to this, the second, operation of the understanding. The argument here is short and direct: if I am indifferent to certain objects, then discovering a causal relationship between them will not raise me from this state of indifference. In Hume's words:

> Where the objects themselves do not affect us, their connexion can never give them any influence; and 'tis plain, that as reason is nothing but the discovery of this connexion, it cannot be by its means that the objects are able to affect us. (p. 414)

The conclusion, then, is that reasoning, of itself, never gives rise either to passions or to actions.

Given this first conclusion that reason can never alone "produce any action, or give rise to volition," Hume proceeds to the further conclusion that it is therefore "incapable of preventing volition, or of disputing the preference with any passion or emotion" (pp. 414–15). His argument seems to turn upon an analogy with Newtonian mechanics:

> 'Tis impossible reason cou'd have the latter effect of preventing volition, but by giving an impulse in a contrary direction to our passion; and that impulse, had it operated alone, wou'd have been able to produce volition.
> (p. 414)

The analogy is not very good since it suggests that a stationary

Reason and the Passions

object (e.g., a wall) could not stop a moving object since it is incapable of putting it in motion in the opposite direction. Anyway, this completes Hume's first argument and leads him to announce the thralldom of reason to the passions.

Later in the *Treatise* Hume will cite this argument as showing the perfect inertness of reason. In fact, Hume does not really believe this. A few pages later, Hume makes the following incautious remark:

> Reason, for instance, exerts itself without producing any sensible emotion; and except in the more sublime disquisitions of philosophy, or in the frivolous subtilties of the schools, scarce ever conveys any pleasure or uneasiness. (p. 417)

Hume's "scarce ever" concedes too much, for now it seems that reasoning can raise feelings and they, in turn, may give rise to actions, e.g., committing volumes of school metaphysics to the flames. Thus the dispute between Hume and his opponents shifts to a question of the extent of reason's ability to influence the passions. In a moment we shall see that Hume goes beyond this apparent slip to grant that reason's influence is both extensive and significant.

(2) Hume's second argument, intended to show that reason cannot affect the passions, obviously pleased him, and it is, in fact, perfectly awful. Its variant, which appears in Book III, is no better – it may be worse. Hume starts out from a commonplace and then draws an irrelevant conclusion from it. Using modern terminology, Hume argues that there is a category mistake in saying that reason can oppose the passions. Reason deals with perceptions which have a representative quality – they are ideas that stand for something or at least pretend to. "A passion," Hume tells us, "is an original existence, or, if you will, modification of existence, and contains not any representative quality, which renders it a copy of any other existence or modification" (p. 415). He then concludes his argument in these words:

> 'Tis impossible, therefore, that this passion can be oppos'd by, or be contradictory to truth and reason; since this contradiction consists in the disagreement of ideas, consider'd as copies, with those objects, which they represent. (p. 415)[3]

Reason and the Passions

Being generous, the first part of Hume's argument seems to come to this: reason is a faculty concerned with the truth or falsity of judgments. To speak of reason opposing something therefore means that it considers it false. Passions are not judgments. Therefore, in a strict and literal sense, reason cannot oppose (or for that matter support) a passion. Stated in this modest way, there is little to say against Hume's argument. The difficulty is that Hume proceeds to puff up his conclusion into the much stronger claim that reason *can have no effect on the passions*. But this introduces a wholly new question: whether one mental activity (e.g., reasoning) can cause another to come into existence. For Hume (since anything might be the cause of anything else) this is a matter that can only be settled by an appeal to experience. Even if we forget Hume's special views concerning causality, the question whether reasoning can produce feelings cannot be decided by the kind of argument Hume has produced. That passions like stones – or, at least, most stones – are not representatives, does not bear upon this matter.[4]

Hume's second argument is a disaster. Hume did not see this, but in a fashion characteristic of the *Treatise* he seems to sense that something more must be said on the subject. He recognizes that there are counter-examples to the claim that reasoning cannot affect the passions and he attempts to deal with them. He introduces these reflections as an illustration of the doctrine that reason cannot oppose the passions because the passions are neither true nor false:

> According to this principle, which is so obvious and natural, 'tis only in two senses, that any affection can be call'd unreasonable. First, When a passion, such as hope or fear, grief or joy, despair or security, is founded on the supposition of the existence of objects, which really do not exist. Secondly, When in exerting any passion in action, we chuse means insufficient for the design'd end, and deceive ourselves in our judgment of causes and effects. (p. 416)

There are profound difficulties with this part of Hume's theory. According to Hume, such passions as hope, fear, grief, and joy are simple impressions. Thus when Hume speaks of a given judgment *accompanying* a passion, he must be taken quite literally. For example, at a given moment I might have a feeling of fear accompanied by the belief that the wall is about to fall down upon me. It is now a commonplace among Hume's critics to point out that these two distinct mental events do not amount to the fear *that* the wall is about to fall down upon me. Put somewhat differently, Hume has no right to speak of a passion *founded on* a supposition unless he can explain how the content of a judgment can have a bearing upon the existence or non-existence of a simple passion. I do not think that he offers any such explanation.

It is not, however, my present concern to criticize Hume's specific theory of the passions; I am primarily interested in Hume's account of the relationship between reason and the passions. Now despite his later talk about the "inertness of reason," it is clear that Hume holds that the understanding can have an effect on the passions. If it can do this in *only* two ways, then it can do this in *two* ways. Furthermore, in those areas where reason does have an influence upon the passions, its rule is supreme.

> 'tis impossible, that reason and passion can ever oppose each other, or dispute for the government of the will and actions. The moment we perceive the falsehood of any supposition, or the insufficiency of any means, our passions yield to our reason without any opposition. (p. 416)

Looking back, it first seemed that Hume was positing an unbridgable gulf between reason and the passions; they cannot oppose each other because they never come into contact. But now a position with a wholly different tendency has emerged: over a limited domain, reason (*via* an associated belief) can affect the passions and in that domain, at least, the passions are the slaves of reason. These developments put Hume's critique of the stoic dictum that reason should govern the passions in a new light. We have shifted from the principled question whether reason, of itself, has any such capacity, to the empirical question of just how far this now-admitted influence extends.

In this same context, Hume makes another provocative remark that has elicited abuse from his time to our own:

> 'Tis not contrary to reason to prefer the destruction of the whole world to the scratching of my finger. 'Tis not contrary to reason for me to chuse my total ruin, to prevent the least

uneasiness of an *Indian* or person wholly unknown to me. (p. 416)

Perhaps Hume should be accused of self-indulgently reaching for a rhetorical effect, but the point he is making is merely a repetition of what he has said already. If Hume is right, then *reasoning* can affect the passions in only two ways. It can show that some belief concerning the object of desire is unreasonable or it can show that some proposed means of attaining (or avoiding) an object is unreasonable. We can imagine a person preferring the destruction of the whole world to the scratching of his finger without attributing to him any false beliefs about the nature of the objects (i.e., a destroyed world or a scratched finger) or any false beliefs about possible means for their attainment. In that case, reasoning would have nothing to say concerning the preference and, in precisely this sense, the preference would not be unreasonable.

(3) Yet wouldn't everyone *say* that it is unreasonable to prefer the destruction of the whole world to the scratching of a finger? Of course, people speak in this way, and I think that Hume might even acknowledge that they *believe* this too. Though false, such a belief is entirely natural.

> Now 'tis certain, there are certain calm desires and tendencies, which, tho' they be real passions, produce little emotion in the mind, and are more known by their effects than by the immediate feeling or sensation. . . When any of these passions are calm, and cause no disorder in the soul, they are very readily taken for the determinations of reason, and are suppos'd to proceed from the same faculty, with that, which judges of truth and falsehood. Their nature and principles have been suppos'd the same, because their sensations are not evidently different. (p. 417)

It may seem extraordinary for Hume to attribute an endemic commitment to falsehood to all of the vulgar and most of the learned, but such an imputation is perfectly consonant with Hume's general approach. We should remind ourselves that Hume not only says that many of our everyday beliefs are unfounded (e.g., that the future will resemble the past), but that many of them are simply false (e.g., that the objects we perceive have a distinct and continued existence). For Hume, consensus in false-

Reason and the Passions

hood – as well as instinctive consensus in unfounded belief – serves as a surrogate for a shared access to truth.

Hume tells us that reason *is* the slave of the passions. We have seen that he does not altogether mean what he says. His more careful view is that reason is limited to two roles in controlling or directing the passions: the identification of objects and the assessment of means for attaining (or avoiding) them. The main implication of this claim is that reason has no place in selecting the ultimate objects of desire or ends of action. This, I think, is the main skeptical move in Hume's treatment of the passions as it occurs in the *Treatise*.

Hume also says that reason *ought only to be* the slave of the passions. He never tells us why. Of course, the phrase may simply be a throwaway, saying nothing more than this: since reason is the slave of the passions, it is idle (hence improper) to assign it any other task. This at least makes some sense out of the word "only" as it appears in the sentence. But I rather think that Hume is here speaking in an ordinary way and saying that it is not only a fact, but also a good thing that our passions are not under the governance of reason. Given the job, reason would botch it. The deprecation of reason is, after all, a persistent theme in Hume's writings. Concerning the skeptic's doubts about the existence of body, he remarks:

> Nature has not left this to his choice, and has doubtless esteem'd it an affair of too great importance to be trusted to our uncertain reasonings and speculations. (p. 187)

He expresses a similar sentiment concerning causal reasoning in the *Enquiry*:

> as this operation of the mind, by which we infer like effects from like causes, and *vice versa*, is so essential to the subsistence of all human creatures, it is not probable, that it could be trusted to the fallacious deductions of our reason, which is slow in its operations; appears not, in any degree, during the first years of infancy; and at best is, in every age and period of life, extremely liable to error and mistake. (p. 55)

And the same position is taken with respect to Hume's most radical skepticism, i.e., his skepticism with regard to reason:

Reason and the Passions

> Most fortunately it happens, that since reason is incapable of dispelling these clouds, nature herself suffices to that purpose, and cures me of this philosophical melancholy and delirium. (p. 269)

Hume constantly reminds us that reason is too fragile a vessel to hold – or too thin a reed to bear – the weighty concerns of life.

I think that Hume adopts the very same attitude toward reason's pretensions to guide the passions. The control of our passions (and hence of our conduct) is too important to be left to a faculty that is "extremely liable to error and mistake." This, I believe, is Hume's position and I suggest that it is this thought that lies in back of the expression "ought only to be" in his critique of the stoic dictum. I shall not claim that this suggestion can be documented conclusively by citing text of the *Treatise* itself. The viewpoint is, however, presented in an essay published shortly after the appearance of the *Treatise*. It is entitled "The Sceptic" and is found in the second volume of *Essays, Moral and Political*, published in 1742. I think that this essay is an important aid for understanding both Hume's account of the relationship between reason and the passions as presented in Book II and his account of the relationship between reason and morals as developed in Book III.

It should be acknowledged from the start that "The Sceptic" has a problematic status which may account for the almost universal tendency of Hume scholars either to treat it gingerly or to ignore it altogether. A few words about the essay's pedigree are, then, in order. "The Sceptic" is the last of four philosophical portraits intended, as Hume tells us in a note to the first essay, "not so much to explain accurately the sentiments of the ancient sects of philosophy, as to deliver the sentiments of sects, that naturally form themselves in the world, and entertain different ideas of human life and of happiness."[5] The first three essays are entitled "The Epicurean," "The Stoic," and "The Platonist." It is plain that the first three essays, despite certain particular points of agreements (notably in "The Stoic"), are not expressive of Hume's own position. Indeed, the Advertisement to the *Essays* contains a remark that suggests that none of these pieces is intended to put forward the author's own opinions:

> 'Tis proper to inform the READER, that, in those ESSAYS, intitled, the Epicurean, Stoic, etc., a certain Character is

personated; and therefore, no Offence ought to be taken at any Sentiments contain'd in them.⁶

Yet despite this disclaimer, I think that "The Sceptic" represents Hume's position in everything but tone and minor detail. Since I shall invoke the aid of this essay here and again in discussing Hume's treatment of morals, let me say something in support of this claim.

Concerning style, Green and Grose have noticed first the similarity between the writing in "The Sceptic" and the writing in Hume's standard works:

> whereas in the companion Essays Hume adopted a high-flown style which is unique in his writings, in 'The Sceptic' he returns to that sober and quiet English, which was not more in accordance with the immediate occasion, than with his habitual tone of thought.⁷

The author of Book I, Part IV of the *Treatise* did not have to affect the formulas and mannerisms of a skeptic. More pointedly, Green and Grose notice that whereas the first three essays are "dismissed without comment":

> a note is added to 'The Sceptic' for the express purpose of setting out the whole truth, in which the preceding paragraphs are only corrected because they are incomplete.⁸

That is, in an *amplitive* note, Hume unquestionably speaks in his own voice, and not in the voice of the "personated" skeptic, and gives these views a further development. Indeed, Hume seems to enter the scene twice in his own person. He begins another amplitive footnote expounding a doctrine also found in the *Treatise* with these words:

> Were I not afraid of appearing too philosophical, I should remind my reader of that famous doctrine, supposed to be fully proved in modern times [i.e., the doctrine of secondary qualities].⁹

Though not entirely forced, it seems more natural to take this remark to the reader – especially given its content – as expressing Hume's viewpoint. If so, we have a second instance of Hume speaking in his own voice in order to develop and support the position presented in the text by the personated skeptic.

Reason and the Passions

We may notice also that some of the passages in "The Sceptic" are strikingly similar to those found in the *Treatise*. The comparison between moral qualities and secondary qualities – the point of the footnote just mentioned – is one example[10] and there are many others. I shall mention only one more. At the close of Book I of the *Treatise* Hume wonders why, after finding that philosophizing inexorably drives him to a despairing skepticism, he should continue to philosophize. His answer is that in certain privileged moments he is naturally inclined to do so:

> These sentiments spring up naturally in my present disposition; and shou'd I endeavour to banish them, by attaching myself to any other business or diversion, I *feel* I shou'd be a loser in point of pleasure; and this is the origin of my philosophy. (p. 271)

Hume's personated skeptic puts it this way:

> To reduce life to exact rule and method, is commonly a painful, oft a fruitless occupation: And is it not also a proof, that we overvalue the prize for which we contend? Even to reason so carefully concerning it, and to fix with accuracy its just idea, would be overvaluing it, were it not that, to some tempers, this occupation is one of the most amusing, in which life could possibly be employed.[11]

Texts of this kind – and many others can be found – show that Hume is here presenting himself under the thinnest possible disguise.

The most important point, however, is that "The Sceptic" is written from the perspective of a *moral sense* theory of precisely the kind developed in the third Book of the *Treatise*. But, of course, even this similarity would not be decisive if it could be shown that there are important differences in doctrine between this essay and the *Treatise*. I claim that there are none, but, of course, it is difficult to establish a negative thesis of this kind. I suspect that anyone who thinks that there are important differences between "The Sceptic" and the corresponding portions of the *Treatise* will also object to the central role that I assign to the skeptical arguments in the *Treatise* itself. If so, this is a better place to fix the disagreement. In any case, in what follows, I shall start with views that are plainly common to "The Sceptic" and the *Treatise* and then show how the development in "The Sceptic" can help us understand why Hume thought that reason *ought* only to be the slave of the passions.

The *Treatise* talks about passions first, and then goes on to examine morals. "The Sceptic" reverses this order, by beginning with the more popular topic of morals. The burden of the first part of the discussion is to establish that "objects have absolutely no worth or value themselves"[12] and therefore values cannot be ascertained by the operations of reasoning upon these objects. This is a central doctrine of the *Treatise* and I shall examine it in detail in the chapter following this. The second half of the essay is dedicated to showing that

> Whoever considers, without prejudice, the course of human actions, will find, that mankind are almost entirely guided by constitution and temper, and that general maxims have little influence, so far as they affect our taste or sentiment.[13]

To affect our lives, reasoning must affect our passions, and this, according to the Sceptic, can only be accomplished in "an indirect manner."[14] In particular, philosophizing may, to some extent, alter our passions by changing our *viewpoint* concerning the object of a passion. In Hume's words:

> a philosopher may step in, and suggest particular views, and considerations, and circumstances, which otherwise would have escaped us; and, by that means, he may either moderate or excite any particular passion.[15]

For example, our sorrow at the loss of a dear friend may be moderated by the thought that his death terminated the intense pain of an incurable illness. We have seen that it is part of the doctrine of the *Treatise* that a change in belief concerning the object of a passion can bring about a change in the passion itself. The idea that an alteration in viewpoint can bring about a change in passion is simply a variation on this idea. With a change in viewpoint, we come to see that an object not only has certain qualities which give rise to particular passions, but also has other qualities whose recognition can elicit still other passions which, in various ways, can modify our original response.

"The Sceptic" contains a theory of the way in which a change in belief can bring about a change in attitude, but the rhetorical point of the essay is not to elaborate this doctrine, but to point out that philosophical thought, i.e., abstruse reflection, can have little effect in this way.

> It may seem unreasonable absolutely to deny authority of philosophy in this respect: But it must be confessed, that there lies this strong presumption against it, that, if these views be natural and obvious, they would have occurred of themselves, without the assistance of philosophy; if they be not natural, they never can have any influence on the affections.[16]

As monitors of the passions, refined reflections suffer either from being overly subtle (and therefore ineffective) or from being too general (and therefore over-inclusive). The following example illustrates both points:

> *Nothing can be more destructive*, says FONTENELLE, *to ambition, and the passion for conquest, than the true system of astronomy. What a poor thing is even the whole globe in comparison of the infinite extent of nature?* This consideration is evidently too distant ever to have any effect. Or, if it had any, would it not destroy patriotism as well as ambition?[17]

Philosophy can avoid the problem of subtlety by drawing its considerations from common life, but even here it will be dogged by the problem of over-inclusiveness. The plain man knows that life is short and uncertain and reflection upon this fact has a tendency to mortify the passions. The difficulty is that all passions tend to be mortified by this reflection – not just those in need of correction and control:

> Such a reflection certainly tends to mortify all our passions: But does it not thereby counterwork the artifice of nature, who has happily deceived us into an opinion, that human life is of some importance? And may not such a reflection be employed with success by voluptuous reasoners, in order to lead us from the paths of action and virtue, into the flowery fields of indolence and pleasure?[18]

Toward the end of the essay, Hume, speaking in his own voice, adds a dozen more considerations drawn from daily life "whose truth is undeniable, and whose natural tendency is to tranquillize and soften all the passions."[19] In the end, however, Hume is no more sanguine than his personated Sceptic about the general effectiveness of these maxims to control our feelings and actions:

> where any real, affecting incident happens; when passion is awakened, fancy agitated, example draws, and counsel urges; the philosopher is lost in the man, and he seeks in vain for that persuasion which before seemed so firm and unshaken.[20]

As a remedy for this, we may have recourse to the writings of entertaining (!) moralists, e.g., to "the wit of Seneca, the gaiety of Montaigne, the sublimity of Shaftesbury," and then by habit and study we may acquire a philosophical temper that gives force to these writings and "by rendering a great part of [our] happiness independent, takes off the edge from all disorderly passions, and tranquillizes the mind."[21] This is surely a very modest role to assign reason in the conduct of life, and even it, if it proves effective, is mostly a matter of happy circumstance. Hume concludes his commentary with a summary statement hardly different in import from the Sceptic's view that he is ostensibly modifying and correcting: "Despise not these helps; but confide not too much in them neither; unless nature has been favourable in the temper, with which she had endowed you."[22]

I think that we can now see an almost exact parallel between Hume's views concerning reason's role in fixing belief and his views concerning reason's role in affecting the passions. First, to the extent that reasoning is abstruse and subtle, it will lack liveliness and, therefore, have no lasting significant effect. Furthermore, in those rare moments when we can follow reason to its most sublime heights, we find ourselves stripped both of all beliefs and of all passions. I do not know whether Hume had these thoughts in mind when he wrote that reason *ought only to be the slave of the passions*, but these are his thoughts and they make sense of this remark.

X

REASON AND MORALS

Although the passions are not an obvious topic for skeptical consideration, morality, the subject of Book III of the *Treatise*, has always been a favorite target of skeptical attack. We shall see that in this area, as in others, Hume develops an *epistemological* skepticism that is wholly unmitigated. He will hold that our moral distinctions cannot be established by any method of reasoning whatsoever. But before examining these skeptical arguments in detail, I wish to note one argument for ethical skepticism that he avoids, for its absence, like the hounds that did not bark, is significant.

The most common (and probably the most persuasive) argument for ethical skepticism proceeds from the apparent fact of ethical diversity or variation: people at different times and in different places have adopted different and often incompatible moral codes. Paralleling a line of argument that is often used to generate perceptual skepticism, it is then argued that there is no rational basis for selecting one moral principle or moral code over any other. Finally, the conclusion is drawn that there can be no rational basis for any moral commitment, including, of course, one's own.[1] The same line of argument is used with respect to aesthetic judgments or judgments of taste, where, as Hume remarks, "common sense, which is so often at variance with philosophy, especially with the sceptical kind, is found, in one instance at least, to agree in pronouncing the same decision."[2]

But however popular and persuasive the argument from diversity might be, Hume does not adopt it. The reasons for this are instructive, for, once more, they show the interplay between skeptical and naturalistic themes in his philosophy. To begin with, Hume has no objections to the skeptical conclusion of this argument, for he will reach conclusions equally radical using different arguments of his own. Instead, he objects to the leading premise of the argument from ethical diversity, for it runs counter to one of his central methodological principles, i.e., that moral phenomena exhibit sufficient orderliness to make the affairs of common life manageable and a circumspect science of man possible.

Hume recognized the importance of this assumption for his program and in various places defended it against particular challenges. This is the central theme of his essay "That Politics may be Reduced to a Science." Here, for example, Hume responds to those who think that the study of political science is idle because the behavior of a society depends so much on the idiosyncrasies of those who govern it. Against this, Hume replies:

> So great is the force of laws, and of particular forms of government, and so little dependence have they on the humours and tempers of men, that consequences almost as general and certain may sometimes be deduced from them, as any which the mathematical sciences afford us.[3]

Again, in his examination of *national character*, Hume stresses cross-cultural similarities among people who play corresponding roles in society.

> The same principle of moral causes fixes the character of different professions, and alters even that disposition, which the particular members receive from the hand of nature. A *soldier* and a *priest* are different characters, in all nations, and all ages; and this difference is founded on circumstances, whose operation is eternal and unalterable.[4]

In the *Treatise*, Hume's insistence upon the uniformity and regularity of moral phenomena comes out most clearly in the section entitled "Of Liberty." Negatively, Hume treats the idea of liberty as fantastic. Equating it with chance, he dismisses it in these words:

> As chance is commonly thought to imply a contradiction, and

Reason and Morals

is at least directly contrary to experience, there are always the same arguments against liberty or free-will. (p. 407)

The positive and more important point of this discussion is that "the *union* betwixt motives and actions has the same constancy, as that in any natural operations . . ." (p. 404). In the *Enquiry* Hume adopts a different line concerning liberty – he no longer attacks the doctrine of liberty but, instead, suggests that liberty and necessity, properly understood, are compatible. This attempted reconciliation has attracted some recent attention,[5] but the central point of this section of the *Enquiry* (Section VIII) is the same as that found in the discussion of liberty and necessity in the *Treatise*: Hume insists that human behavior exhibits a sufficient degree of uniformity to allow causal judgments to be made concerning it. As Hume sees it, the very possibility of the science of man depends upon this uniformity.

> What would become of *history*, had we not a dependence on the veracity of the historian according to the experience which we have had of mankind? How could *politics* be a science, if laws and forms of government had not a uniform influence upon society? Where would be the foundations of *morals*, if particular characters had no certain or determinate power to produce particular sentiments, and if these sentiments had no constant operation on actions?[6]

The final sentence in the above passage brings us back to morals and points to another reason why Hume is eager to minimize the extent of moral disagreement. Actually, the mere fact of disagreement carries no skeptical (or anti-uniformitarian) consequences when we have some objective standard for deciding which opinions are right and which are wrong. Speaking in the common way, we can test our judgments about the world by checking to see whether the world is the way we say it is. But on a moral (and aesthetic) *sense* theory of the kind that Hume champions, there is nothing in the object to serve as a check upon the correctness of our moral (or aesthetic) judgments. For example, that people have differing and discordant views concerning the nature of the universe in no way threatens the objectivity of natural science. Those who disagree with the findings of natural science are simply wrong in their opinions, and *the facts show this*. Of course, this naive appeal to facts is itself subject to skeptical attack, but the point is that such an attack must go deeper than one against a position that does not even pretend to an objective basis for judgment. This difference comes out in the following passage from "The Sceptic":

> If I examine the PTOLOMAIC and COPERNICAN systems, I endeavour only, by my enquiries, to know the real situation of the planets; that is, in other words, I endeavor to give them, in my conception, the same relations, that they bear towards each other in the heavens. To this operation of the mind, therefore, there seems to be always a real, though often an unknown standard, in the nature of things; nor is truth or falsehood variable by the various apprehensions of mankind. Though all human race should for ever conclude, that the sun moves, and the earth remains at rest, the sun stirs not an inch from his place for all these reasonings; and such conclusions are eternally false and erroneous.
>
> But the case is not the same with the qualities of *beautiful and deformed, desirable and odious*, as with truth and falsehood. In the former case, the mind is not content with merely surveying its objects, as they stand in themselves: It also feels a sentiment of delight or uneasiness, approbation or blame, consequent to that survey; and this sentiment determines it to affix the epithet *beautiful or deformed, desirable or odious*. Now, it is evident, that this sentiment must depend upon the particular fabric or structure of the mind, which enables such particular forms to operate in such a particular manner, and produces a sympathy or conformity between the mind and its objects. Vary the structure of the mind or inward organs, the sentiment no longer follows, though the form remains the same.[7]

Since, as Hume concludes, "objects have absolutely no worth or value in themselves," these objects cannot serve as an independent standard for the correctness or incorrectness of our moral judgments. It is for this reason that a moral sense theory is *particularly* susceptible to the standard argument for ethical skepticism, i.e., the argument for the diversity of moral opinion. The only response that Hume has – and as far as I can see *can* have – is to deny that this diversity is as extreme as the relativist in ethics

Reason and Morals

would have it. This response comes out in a passage which was noticed briefly earlier. In a footnote to "The Sceptic," Hume compares moral qualities with secondary qualities, citing the modern doctrine that such secondary qualities as colors do not "lie in the object."

> The case is the same with beauty and deformity, virtue and vice. This doctrine, however, takes off no more from the reality of the latter qualities, than from that of the former; nor need it give any umbrage either to critics or moralists. Tho' colours were allowed to lie only in the eye, would dyers or painters ever be less regarded or esteemed? *There is a sufficient uniformity in the senses and feelings of mankind, to make all these qualities the objects of art and reasoning, and to have the greatest influence on life and manners.*[8]

The implication of the closing sentence in this passage is plain: if human responses were highly variable and inconstant, then the activities of daily life and the possibility of a science of man would both be subverted. Over against this abstract possibility, we find only a brute fact of nature: "there is a sufficient uniformity in the senses and feelings of mankind" to support the activities of daily life and thus to provide a subject matter for the science of man.

One feature, then, of Hume's skepticism concerning morals is that it avoids the popular and persuasive argument from diversity. It does so because strengthening the premise of that argument undercuts one of Hume's basic methodological principles: nature, including human nature, is, on the whole, tolerably uniform. A second feature of Hume's skeptical position is that his arguments are largely shaped by the specific targets they are aimed against. In particular, Hume is *most* eager to refute various versions of ethical rationalism that attempt to treat ethical propositions on an analogy with mathematical propositions. Yet, in the end, Hume's critique of the place of reason in ethics rises to the highest generality. Although Hume had quite specific models of ethical rationalism in mind as he formulated his criticisms, the object of his attack is the pretension of the faculty of reason itself, not the pretension of this or that philosopher.

Having said all this, it is disappointing, when turning to the text, to discover that much of the discussion is obscure and that some of Hume's arguments are embarrassingly weak. Here is the

Reason and Morals

way in which Hume poses the fundamental question that will give shape to his discussion.

> Now as perceptions resolve themselves into two kinds, viz. *impressions* and *ideas*, this distinction gives rise to a question, with which we shall open up our present enquiry concerning morals, *Whether 'tis by means of our* ideas *or* impressions *we distinguish betwixt vice and virtue, and pronounce an action blameable or praise-worthy?* (p. 456)

First of all, Hume has chosen a curious way of posing this, his basic, question. From the first part of the *Treatise* we know that impressions are supposed to give rise to ideas, these ideas being fainter copies of the original impressions. So if moral distinctions arise from original impressions, we would then expect there to be moral ideas as well. Yet Hume here seems to be presenting us with a choice: either impressions or ideas. In fact, Hume avoids the use of the expressions "moral ideas" and "moral beliefs."

We can get a better understanding of the form of Hume's inquiry by noticing how he makes his question more specific. Speaking rather narrowly of the theories he is most eager to reject, he says: "All these systems concur in the opinion, that morality, like truth, is discern'd merely by ideas, and by their juxta-position and comparison" (pp. 456–7). Here the discussion focuses on theories that treat moral judgments as relations of ideas. On Hume's account of such judgments, their truth can be determined through reasoning alone, i.e., through the juxtaposition and comparison of ideas. Later, Hume will extend his inquiry to ask whether moral judgments concern matters of fact about the quality of an action or the character of an agent. He will argue that they do not. Anyway, I think that we can now see the point of Hume's question: he is asking whether our moral apprehensions arise *immediately* as impressions or are the result of *reasoning* of some kind.

The opening section of Book III contains three (perhaps four) arguments intended to show that moral distinctions are not discerned through reasoning. The first turns upon the supposed passivity of reason. The second concerns the proper object of reason – representations, not real existents. Both of these arguments are prefigured in Book II. The text also contains a third argument which closely parallels Hume's famous skeptical argu-

Reason and Morals

ment concerning induction. It is intended to show that moral questions cannot be settled either by demonstrative reasoning or through reasoning concerning cause and effect. The text may also contain a fourth argument dealing with the supposed underivability of an *ought* from an *is*. This is sometimes read as a distinct *meta*-ethical argument, but I shall argue that it is better not to read it this way.

The central claim of the first argument is that "reason is perfectly inert" (p. 458). To support this claim, Hume relies upon his earlier discussion in Book II. He then argues as follows:

> Morals excite passions, and produce or prevent actions.
> Reason of itself is utterly impotent in this particular. The rules of morality, therefore, are not conclusions of our reason. (p. 457)

This is not an altogether easy argument to interpret, for the crucial expression "of itself" is obscure. Here is one interpretation of the argument that proceeds validly from principles that Hume accepts:

> A moral apprehension excites passions and produces (or prevents) actions.
> A rational apprehension, of itself, does not excite passions and produce (or prevent) actions.
> Therefore a moral apprehension is not simply a rational apprehension.

Stated this way, the argument strikes me as valid, so we may ask how the rationalist in morals would respond to the premises. The second premise was presumably established in Book II. Now here, in Book III, Hume speaks rather cavalierly about having shown that reason is perfectly inert, but under close scrutiny, we saw that the text contains a complex view concerning the relationship between reasoning and the passions. It simply is not true – as some of Hume's loose writing suggests – that reasoning can have *no* effect upon the passions. Hume's more careful view is that reason can affect the passions only in two ways – either by identifying an object of some passion or by finding some means for its attainment or avoidance. Thus, in the absence of any principled gulf between reason and the passions, the rationalist is free to argue that the apprehension of the moral fittingness of an action is a *third* way in which the operation of reason can give rise to passions and (hence) actions. This is either true or false as the case may be, but, as far as I can see, nothing Hume says in this part of his critique of rationalist ethics is responsive to this obvious retort. In any case, I shall not dwell upon this point since the ethical rationalist has a much simpler defense against Hume's attack.

The ethical rationalist can more plausibly reject the first premise of Hume's argument, i.e., he can deny that a moral apprehension can excite a passion and thereby give rise to (or prevent) action. He could argue as follows:[9] "Understanding deals with the moral characteristics of an action in the same way that it deals with other (non-moral) characteristics. Through the employment of the understanding we are able to ascertain whether an action possesses or lacks a particular moral characteristic. This of itself does not move us to action, but human beings possess, to a greater or lesser extent, a desire to perform actions that are morally fitting and a desire to shun actions that are morally unfitting. It is in virtue of these desires that our moral apprehensions are connected with actions." In sum, the moral rationalist can show how moral apprehension is connected to action by invoking the following practical syllogism:

This action has the characteristic of being morally sound.
I have a desire to perform actions that are morally sound.
I shall, therefore, (have at least a tendency to) perform this action.

In his turn, Hume cannot simply deny that actions possess moral characteristics, for that is the very point at issue. Nor does it seem that he could make a persuasive case for the claim that we do not desire to perform actions *because* they are morally sound. The issue would turn upon a very nice distinction: is a moral apprehension already a feeling or desire, as Hume would have it, or a quality in actions that call forth desires, as the moral rationalist could maintain? Hume posits a *specifically moral feeling* and *via* this feeling secures a connection between a moral apprehension (i.e., a feeling) and action. The moral rationalist posits a *specifically moral quality* and then secures a connection with action by introducing a desire to perform actions that possess this quality. Since a connection between moral apprehension and action is secured in both cases, we are left to choose between specifically moral feelings or specifically moral qualities. If Hume's argument

Reason and Morals

from the "inertness of reason" resolves itself into this question, then his purposes would be better served by avoiding this argument and approaching the issue more directly.

Although Hume put great store in this argument from the supposed inertness of reason, he adds others that are aimed more directly against the doctrine that our moral judgments are established through reasoning. His second argument, like his first, made its initial appearance in Book II. The Book III version is spelled out in the following way:

> Reason is the discovery of truth or falshood. Truth or falshood consists in an agreement or disagreement either to the *real* relations of ideas, or to *real* existence and matter of fact. Whatever, therefore, is not susceptible of this agreement or disagreement, is incapable of being true or false, and can never be an object of our reason. Now 'tis evident our passions, volitions, and actions, are not susceptible of any such agreement or disagreement; being original facts and realities, compleat in themselves, and implying no reference to other passions, volitions, and actions. 'Tis impossible, therefore, they can be pronounced either true or false, and be either contrary or conformable to reason. (p. 458)

On one reading this is a good argument directed against a weak position which, perhaps, no one held. On a second reading, which I am afraid the text supports, this is a perfectly dreadful argument directed against the traditional position that Hume, in fact, wishes to refute. On the first reading, Hume merely leads an imagined opponent into the following solecism:

> Certain actions are contrary to reason.
> Whatever is contrary to reason is false.
> Therefore, certain actions are false.

Any system of morals that leads to this category mistake deserves all the scorn that Hume heaps upon it. It is, however, doubtful that the theories that Hume was most eager to refute (those of the Cambridge Platonists and of Samuel Clarke) actually contained this blunder. To be fair to Hume, it must be said that some of the loose writing of these philosophers invites just this criticism. Speaking of Clarke, Sidgwick remarks that

> his anxiety to exhibit the parallelisms between ethical and mathematical truth . . . renders his general terminology inappropriate and occasionally leads him into downright extravagances. *E.g.*, it is patently absurd to say that "a man who willfully acts contrary to Justice wills things to be what they are not and cannot be".[10]

Of course, such extravagance demands correction, but it is easily made without changing anything essential to the rationalist's position. For example, the above argument leading to its absurd conclusion can be made right by the following rephrasing:

> Certain moral judgments are contrary to reason.
> Whatever is contrary to reason is false.
> Therefore, certain moral judgments are false.

In this new form, the argument no longer leads to a conclusion that is absurd upon its face. Since the premises of this new argument reasonably characterize views held by ethical rationalists, Hume's attack taken this way has not refuted that position, only corrected its talk.

Yet as we look at that text, it is hard to avoid the impression that Hume thinks he has established a much stronger thesis than anything canvassed so far. He plainly suggests that reason cannot be used to resolve moral issues just because passions, volitions, and actions are not themselves representatives, i.e., things that pretend to be either true or false. More briefly: reason deals only with things that are true or false, and actions (passions, etc.) are neither. This is the second (and surely more literal) reading of the text. And if this is, in fact, what Hume wishes to maintain, then Harrison is right in replying that "one might just as well argue that, since reason discovers what is true or false, reason cannot discover whether the earth is round or flat, or being round or flat would consist in being true or false."[11] Indeed, it seems that Hume is here involved in a linguistic muddle far deeper than those that arise in the careless talk of his opponents.

The text gives no sign that Hume saw any weakness or incompleteness in his arguments from the inertness of reason and from the supposed inappropriateness of saying that an action can be contrary to reason. Nonetheless, he adds a *third* argument intended to show that "thought and understanding" are not "alone capable of fixing the boundaries of right and wrong" (p. 463). This is a genuinely skeptical argument, for it adduces epistemological reasons intended to show that moral judgments cannot be established either as relations of ideas or as matters of fact. It is also a far more interesting argument than the two embarrassingly weak arguments just canvassed.

The argument is put forward in the form of a dilemma:

> If the thought and understanding were alone capable of fixing the boundaries of right and wrong, the character of virtuous and vicious either must lie in some relations of objects, or must be a matter of fact, which is discovered by our reasoning. This consequence is evident. As the operations of human understanding divide themselves into two kinds, the comparing of ideas, and the inferring of matter of fact; were virtue discover'd by the understanding; it must be an object of one of these operations, nor is there any third operation of the understanding, which can discover it. (p. 463)

The wording here is interesting, for except for the fact that Hume speaks of "relations of objects" rather than "relations to ideas," the argument has the pattern of Hume's skepticism concerning induction as it appears in the *Enquiry*. This pattern of argument is certainly implicit in Book I of the *Treatise* but here, for the first time, Hume's Fork makes a transparent appearance at the beginning of a skeptical argument.

Turning to the first alternative, Hume speaks of "an opinion very industriously propagated by certain philosophers, that morality is susceptible of demonstration" (p. 463). For understandable historical reasons, Hume spends most of his time attacking this first option. His reasoning roughly parallels the previous argument intended to show that inductive inferences are not demonstrative. Actually, the argument is a bit stronger in one way, but weaker in another. Hume's argument against the demonstrative character of causal inference depended, in part, upon the claim that there are only *four* relations "susceptible of certainty and demonstration," i.e., resemblance, contrariety, degrees in quality, and proportions in quantity and number. He then argued, with some plausibility, that causal inferences could not be reduced to inferences depending upon these four relationships. The argument, of course, is no stronger than the unsupported claim that there are only these four relations which are susceptible of certainty and demonstration. The argument concerning *moral* relations begins in the same way, but improves on the earlier argument by not relying quite as much upon the assertion that the list of relations that admit of demonstration is *complete*. Beginning with a reference to these four relations, Hume reasons as follows:

> If you assert, that vice and virtue consist in relations susceptible of certainty and demonstration, you must confine yourself to those *four* relations, which alone admit of that degree of evidence; and in that case you run into absurdities, from which you will never be able to extricate yourself. For as you make the very essence of morality to lie in the relations, and as there is no one of these relations but what is applicable, not only to an irrational, but also to an inanimate object; it follows, that even such objects must be susceptible of merit or demerit. (pp. 463–4)

A few pages later, Hume illustrates this point by comparing an act of parricide with the case of an oak or elm which "by the dropping of its seed . . . produces a sapling below it, which springing up by degrees, at last overtops and destroys the parent tree" (p. 467). Here all the relevant relations seem the same, yet we find the act of parricide vicious, whereas the sapling's activity merely indifferent.

Of course, the argument, so far stated, depends upon the claim that there are four and only four relations susceptible of certainty and demonstration. Yet Hume does a bit better here than in his discussion of causal inferences in answering this criticism. Not only does he challenge his opponent to produce another such relation, he antecedently lays down a criterion of adequacy that any candidate must meet:

> As moral good and evil belong only to the actions of the mind, and are deriv'd from our situation with regard to external objects, the relations, from which these moral distinctions arise, must lie only betwixt internal actions, and external objects, and must not be applicable either to internal actions, compared among themselves, or to external objects, when placed in opposition to other external objects. . . . Now it

seems difficult to imagine, that any relation can be discover'd betwixt our passions, volitions and actions, compared to external objects, which relation might not belong either to these passions and volitions, or to these external objects, compar'd among *themselves*. (pp. 464–5)

This same argument could not have been used with respect to causal inferences because it is an important feature of Hume's treatment of causality that causal relations can hold between any two kinds of events whatsoever.

Even though this argument sets forth a legitimate challenge, it is not hard to imagine how the moral rationalist would answer it. The relation they claim to recognize between an agent and a certain line of conduct in a given situation is moral *fittingness* (or something of the kind). They would agree that this relationship cannot be reduced to the four relations given by Hume for, indeed, this relation cannot be reduced to any combination of non-moral relations. Moral fittingness is *sui generis*. When asked to explain why this relation holds between human beings and certain lines of conduct and not between inanimate objects, the rationalist can simply declare that this is a primitive feature of the kind of relation.[12] This may seem a weak reply, but the moral sense theorist must give much the same answer when asked why actions of human beings alone arouse our moral sentiments.

Before moving on to the second half of Hume's *third* argument, I wish to consider another curious omission that is of far greater consequence. Early in the *Treatise*, Hume divided knowledge into two categories: *intuition* and *demonstration*, yet in the present discussion he never considers the possibility that moral relations are *intuitively* ascertained. This is a curious omission because intuitionism is the most common form that ethical rationalism takes. More pointedly, the Cambridge Platonists and Samuel Clarke were certainly intuitionists. Hume seems not to have considered the position he was most eager to refute.

Hume spends most of his time attacking those who treat moral apprehension on an analogy with the apprehension of mathematical truths. But he is careful to give his position complete generality by adding a second argument intended to show that morality "consists not of any *matter of fact*, which can be discover'd by the understanding." "This," he says, "is the *second* part of our argument; and if it can be made evident, we may conclude, that morality is not an object of reason" (p. 468). The argument also has wider importance, for here, for the first time, Hume addresses himself directly to the question whether moral properties are objective characteristics of actions. Without a strongly defended negative answer to this question all the previous arguments are ineffective. For example, if moral properties are objective characteristics of actions, then the moral rationalists need only invoke a desire to perform actions that possess these characteristics in order to show how moral apprehension is linked to action. Again, if moral properties are objective characteristics of actions, the rationalist in ethics can concede that moral truths are not established demonstratively, and then claim instead that they are the object of a *sui generis* intuition. The argument, then, is important for Hume's purposes. It is also brief, loosely constructed, and subject to competing interpretations. The central passage reads as follows:

> can there be any difficulty in proving, that vice and virtue are not matters of fact, whose existence we can infer by reason? Take any action allow'd to be vicious: Wilful murder, for instance. Examine it in all lights, and see if you can find that matter of fact, or real existence, which you call *vice*. In whichever way you take it, you find only certain passions, motives, volitions and thoughts. There is no other matter of fact in the case. The vice entirely escapes you, as long as you consider the object. (p. 468)

This passage is reminiscent of the earlier discussion of necessary connections and, in a somewhat less direct way, of the discussion of the unity and identity of objects. In each case we are asked to view an object in a particular way. We are to view it as it is presented to us: bracketing out all influences of association and feeling. From the perspective of this phenomenalist gaze, all sequences of events will seem unconnected, all properties of objects will appear separate, loose, and perishing, and now, we are told, all actions will strike us as morally insignificant. This is not the natural (everyday) way of viewing the world – the plain man knows nothing about radical empiricism. It is a philosophical perspective we adopt in order to distinguish objective features of events, objects, and actions from those features that are "spread

Reason and Morals

upon them" by the mind. Hume's argument (or claim) is that anyone who adopts this perspective will see at once that no action (in itself) possesses moral characteristics.

Hume next shifts his reflective gaze from the action to our inward response to it. Having concluded that "the vice entirely escapes you, as long as you consider the object," he continues, rather obscurely, in these words:

> You never can find it [i.e., the vice], till you turn your reflexion into your own breast, and find a sentiment of disapprobation, which arises in you, towards this action. Here is a matter of fact; but 'tis the object of feeling, not of reason. It lies in yourself, not in the object. (pp. 468–9)

I do not think that Hume can be taken quite literally here. What he actually says – but can hardly mean – is that the *vice* is discovered in your own breast and consists in your feeling of disapprobation which arises in you toward that action. If vice is in the breast of the beholder, then it is the beholder, not the action beheld, that is vicious. I am sure that Hume does not mean this. What he does mean is that certain feelings are the source of our judgments of moral approbation and moral disapprobation. Without these feelings, human beings would find actions neither morally good nor morally bad. Hume makes this point somewhat awkwardly in the sentence that continues the last cited passage.

> So that when you pronounce any action or character to be vicious, you mean nothing, but that from the constitution of your nature you have a feeling or sentiment of blame from the contemplation of it. (p. 469)

Again I do not think that we ought to take Hume quite literally – or, to be less condescending, I do not think that we should attribute to Hume the technical pretensions that contemporary philosophers put into the word 'mean'. I think that this remark is intended informally and should be read as follows: "So that when you pronounce any action or character to be vicious, you *show* nothing but that from the constitution of your nature you have a feeling or sentiment, etc." Hume is interested in the source of our moral judgments and in explaining this he seems wholly indifferent to the niceties of present meta-ethical discussions. I shall return to this issue at the close of this chapter. In any case, by

Reason and Morals

this two-pronged argument – so similar in its form to his skeptical argument concerning induction – Hume thinks that he has shown that "morality is not an object of reason."[13]

Hume concludes his discussion of the place of reason in ethics with a passage that has a modern ring. Perhaps for this reason, it has attracted much attention and has often been discussed in isolation from its surrounding context. He remarks that when reading works of moral philosophy,

> of a sudden I am surpriz'd to find, that instead of the usual copulations of propositions, *is*, and *is not*, I meet with no proposition that is not connected with an *ought*, or an *ought not*. This change is imperceptible; but is, however, of the last consequence. For as this *ought*, or *ought not*, expresses some new relation or affirmation, 'tis necessary that it should be observ'd and explain'd; and at the same time that a reason should be given, for what seems altogether inconceivable, how this new relation can be a deduction from others, which are entirely different from it. (p. 469)

I do not think that this passage contains a new argument added by Hume to the three just examined. Instead, its intention is to make more vivid the force of the third argument – in particular, the first half of that argument. Loosely put, the passage concerns transitions from an *is* to an *ought*. Hume is not objecting to such transitions: he is not saying that they should not be made. He is inquiring into the basis of such transitions, not rejecting them. He states that this transition cannot be a matter of deduction since it is inconceivable "how this new relation can be a deduction from others, which are entirely different from it." But for this claim to have any force, it must be antecedently shown that the *ought* does indeed introduce a *new* relation or affirmation different from those relations that are the source of demonstrative truths. Hume thinks that he has established this claim earlier by pointing out that there are only four relations that support demonstrative reasoning, and moral relations cannot be reduced to them. Thus, the argumentative force of this passage relies upon the force of this previous argument which, as we have seen, is not particularly persuasive.

In any case, transitions from an *is* to an *ought* do take place and the thrust of Hume's argument is that they are inexplicable on rationalist accounts which attempt to treat them as demonstrative

Reason and Morals

inferences. In contrast, they are perfectly intelligible on Hume's approach. The "ought" is not some new relationship inferred from others, it is expressive of a feeling we have in response to certain situations. The generalized statement of this conclusion is given in the opening sentence of Section II, Book III:

> Thus the course of the argument leads us to conclude, that since vice and virtue are not discoverable merely by reason, or the comparison of ideas, it must be by means of some impression or sentiment they occasion, that we are able to mark the difference betwixt them. Our decisions concerning moral rectitude and depravity are evidently perceptions; and as all perceptions are either impressions or ideas, the exclusion of the one is a convincing argument for the other. Morality, therefore, is more properly felt than judg'd of. (p. 470)

At the close of this passage, Hume returns to the curious wording of his initial question: forgetting that there should be moral ideas as the decaying remnants of moral impressions, he asks us to choose between impressions and ideas. But I think that we now know what he means by this: we are asked to choose between two faculties, understanding and sense. The skeptical arguments are intended to eliminate the understanding from the competition.

The Significance of Moral Judgments. The main point of this work is to further three interrelated theses: (1) Hume is an unmitigated epistemological skeptic – both at large and in particular areas of belief. (2) His prescriptive skepticism is, however, strongly mitigated. (3) His conceptual skepticism is also thoroughly mitigated. This pattern of commitments has emerged again with respect to moral reasoning. Asked for a rational justification of our moral ascriptions, Hume's unqualified answer is that there is none. We can, of course, examine, as an empirical question, the causes of our feeling of moral approbation and moral disapprobation (and most of Book III is dedicated to just this), but if we ask ourselves whether we ought to have such feelings – or whether it is appropriate to have such feelings – once more no rational argument is forthcoming to answer this question. Again in the area of morals, these epistemological reflections do not lead to a recommendation for the suspension of belief or, more pointedly, to a recommendation for a withdrawal from action. It is a brute fact of human nature that certain kinds of actions arouse within us feelings of moral approval and disapproval. It is another fact of human nature that such feelings have a tendency to move us to action. Although skeptical reflection may momentarily distort these natural propensities, nature will always win out and we will again feel and act in our normal and accustomed way.

As always, the matter of Hume's conceptual skepticism is more difficult to understand. Despite his early proclamations that philosophers often use words with no corresponding ideas associated with them, I have argued that Hume is a mitigated conceptual skeptic. Although he sometimes argues that philosophers employ words with no meaning, he more often accuses them of dealing in *fictions*. Broadly speaking, these philosophical fictions are introduced as surrogates for those false belief of common sense which cannot withstand philosophical scrutiny.

Turning to ethics, we do not find the same level of sophistication here that we found, for example, in Part IV of Book I. Yet the main contours of Hume's position concerning *necessary connections*, *substance*, and *moral relations* are strikingly similar. The vulgar believe (quite falsely) that moral qualities are simply observable characteristics of certain actions. In place of this, some among the learned believe (again quite falsely) that the moral qualities of an action consist in its *fittingness*, where this fittingness is not an empirical quality, but, instead, a quality apprehended by reason. The truth of the matter, according to Hume, is that we are no more able to apprehend moral qualities in actions than we are able to perceive necessary connections between events or a substance underlying the properties of an object. Taken in itself – or merely as it is presented – an action will appear as valueless as its aspects will appear separate and loose. Finally, we find something related to a necessary connection or to moral worth when we look within ourselves and notice how the object affects us. The vulgar and most of the learned fall into the natural error of assigning these felt qualities to the objects or actions that occasion them.

But a question remains which a commentator in the twentieth century finds imperative to raise: what, according to Hume, do we *mean* when we say that an action is morally virtuous or morally vicious? Hume says a great deal that bears upon this question, but I do not think that he ever sets about answering it directly.

Reason and Morals

More strongly, in the sense in which we now use the word, Hume does not propound a *meta-ethical* theory.[14] Admittedly, some of Hume's language points to a subjectivist view of the meaning of ethical discourse:

> when you pronounce any action or character to be vicious, you mean nothing, but that from the constitution of your nature you have a feeling or sentiment of blame from the contemplation of it. (p. 469)

Since Hume here speaks of the "meaning" of our ethical pronouncements, it may seem to do violence to the text not to read it in a modern (meta-ethical) way. Yet such a reading runs counter to one of the central points in Hume's moral theory, i.e., that a moral apprehension is not the result of any kind of reasoning. Now read as a definition or as an analysis of moral pronouncements, this sentence implies that our ethical judgments are not simply about our feelings, but also about the dispositional state of our constitution. This is implied by the phrase: "you mean nothing, but that from the constitution of your nature, you have a feeling." But assertions about dispositions are causal, and making causality an ingredient in ethical statements runs counter to one of Hume's central doctrines.

I think that there are a number of passages which, taken at face value, suggest a subjectivist meta-ethical theory. Some other passages suggest an emotivist reading of Hume's position. This passage occurs in his essay "Of the Standard of Taste":

> The word *virtue*, with its equivalent in every tongue, implies praise; as that of *vice* does blame: And no one, without the most obvious and grossest impropriety, could affix reproach to a term, which in general acceptation is understood in a good sense; or bestow applause, where the idiom requires disapprobation.[15]

This is not a theoretical statement of the emotivist position, but it is not far-fetched to suppose that Hume's claim that the word "virtue" implies praise or bestows applause means just that it expresses praise or gives applause.

Perhaps the main reason for *not* associating either emotivism or subjectivism with Hume's moral philosophy is that these positions seem inherently implausible. Both Stroud and Harrison are affected by this consideration.[16] Harrison, for example, argues against the plausibility of all forms of non-cognitivism (which includes emotivism, but not subjectivism) by citing a wide range of similarities that hold between moral sentences and other sentences that plainly are used to express truth claims. But we must ask whether the similarities he cites are significant or merely superficial, and that question can only be answered in the context of a broader theory. Actually, emotivism (or some other version of non-cognitivism) seems quite plausible within Hume's general framework. Whatever else he is saying, Hume insists that moral pronouncements cannot appeal to matters of fact. That is just the point of the third argument examined above. This means that evidence cannot be used to support our moral pronouncements and, if this is so, it is hard to see what the propositional status of a moral pronouncement comes to – or at least why it should be so important to insist upon it.

Furthermore, given the general associationist framework of Hume's position, both subjectivism and emotivism could be used as the basis for explaining how one person's moral apprehensions are related to another's. When I say that something is vicious, I *make known* my feelings either by speaking about them (subjectivism) or by expressing them (emotivism). *Via* sympathy (one of Hume's favorite explanatory notions) this can initiate a train of associations of the very kind that Hume is fond of tracing out. In this way, one person's moral pronouncements can be related to another's. They can at least seem to agree or disagree. I am suggesting, then, that neither subjectivism nor emotivism will seem implausible in the context of a thorough-going associationist philosophy of mind of the type that Hume champions. Indeed, emotivism might be the best meta-ethical theory for his purposes.

It is not my present purpose to take a roll-call of the meta-ethical theories developed in this century and then to ask of each how it would square with the main features of Hume's moral philosophy. Given Hume's associationism, any theory that gives feeling a central place will be a plausible candidate for the job. Furthermore, following Stroud, I think it is a mistake to attribute any specific meta-ethical theory to Hume. Hume trod the way of ideas, not the way of words.[17] Here I am only concerned with natural candidates for meta-ethical companionship with Hume's moral philosophy. Both subjectivism and emotivism will do, but an even better candidate has been nominated by Stroud and Mackie. Here is what Stroud says:

> I contemplate or observe an action or character and then feel a certain sentiment of approbation towards it. In saying or believing that X is virtuous I am indeed ascribing to X itself a certain objective characteristic, even though, according to Hume, there really is no such characteristic to be found 'in' X. In that way virtue and vice are like secondary qualities.

Stroud indicates that my moral judgments may also be said to *express* my approval, but then continuing the above line of thought, he says:

> The judgment is an expression of my feeling, but not a report to the effect that I have such a feeling. Rather, it is the attribution of a certain characteristic – virtue or goodness – to an action or character. Although there is in fact no such characteristic in actions and characters, the feelings we get on contemplating them inevitably lead us to ascribe it to them. ... Our moral judgments ... are 'projections'.[18]

I think that this is a remarkably good suggestion because it meets the immediate needs of Hume's moral philosophy – it is easy to imagine how it could serve as the basis of associationist explanations of moral phenomena – and it does this in a way that invokes one of Hume's favorite ideas, i.e., that the mind "spreads itself" on the objects it contemplates.

All the same, there is something strange about the notion that we project our feelings upon the world – at least the doctrine needs more elaboration than Hume has given it. Approaching the matter flatfootedly, it really does not make sense to attribute my *feelings* to the objects or actions I contemplate. If I feel sad, then the world may strike me as gloomy, and this gloominess may be a projection of my feeling of sadness. I do not, however, suppose that the world possesses this sensation. Gloominess, then, seems to be the form that sadness takes when projected upon the world. In parallel fashion, necessary connectedness may be the form that my feelings of expectation take when projected upon events that I have experienced as constantly conjoined. Moral viciousness may be the form that moral disapprobation takes when it is projected upon an action that arouses this disapproval. And so on. What is needed here is an account of this relationship between feelings and projected qualities. Without this, it will be hard to choose between the position of common sense and that of the projectionist. The deeper wisdom might be that the assignment of certain qualities of consciousness (e.g., colors) is the result of *intro*jecting features of the public world into consciousness.

But whatever the independent merits of the projectionist theory, Stroud is surely right in thinking it consonant both with Hume's moral philosophy and with his broader philosophical position. To pursue this latter point (perhaps further than Stroud), Hume is fond of attributing endemic false beliefs to the plain man. The plain man believes that colors, tastes, scents, etc., reside in objects, but that is false. More pointedly, the plain man believes that the entities he senses have a distinct and continued existence, and that also is false. We are now told that the same species of falsehood infects all of his moral beliefs. The wonder, at this point, is that mankind can survive under the weight of such universally shared falsehood.[19] Hume's answer is that these falsehoods or fictions cause no difficulties and may even be of value just because they are almost universally shared.

Let me use an analogy to illustrate the form of Hume's position. At one time it was universally believed that the sun makes a daily traverse of the sky. We still speak of the sun rising and setting and, for that matter, it does *seem* to move. Yet we now know that such motions are merely apparent. We can imagine a philosopher declaring that all statements to the effect that the sun is rising, setting, reaching its zenith, falling below the yardarm, and so on, are false. This may seem an unsophisticated position, for, as the story now goes, it mistakenly assumes that the plain man is engaged in astronomy when, in fact, his language game is bounded by constraints of daily life quite remote from astronomical considerations. But the sophisticated position is itself fishy. Those unfamiliar with the Copernican theory really do believe that the sun moves, and they cite these motions for practical purposes in just the same way that they cite other motions (e.g., of the tides). And a modern man informed of the Copernican theory will, when asked, admit that his remarks attributing motion to the sun are just false. What he sees, of course, is that this falsehood makes no practical difference. This captures half of Hume's position: that a shared falsehood can be innocent. The other more radical

Reason and Morals

half is that shared falsehood may actually be essential for the survival of creatures such as ourselves.[20]

To bring this discussion to a close, it seems that we may associate a variety of meta-ethical theories with Hume's moral philosophy. Subjectivism, emotivism, and projectionism all find some support in Hume's writings and given the flexibility of his associationism each of these positions fits well enough into Hume's general framework. Indeed, given the associationism Hume advocates, it is not particularly important for him to specify just how our ethical affirmations *make known* our feelings. Perhaps it is for this reason that Hume was able to express his views about moral "pronouncements" in such a casual and, from our point of view at least, incoherent manner.

More importantly, however loose Hume's remarks may strike us, nothing in his discussion of moral pronouncements suggests that he is committed to a conceptual skepticism concerning them. He nowhere suggests that the plain man is speaking without meaning when he calls particular actions either virtuous or vicious. The plain man may not understand the principles that underlie his moral affirmations, but he is not speaking nonsense when he makes them. Furthermore, although the underlying mechanisms are not understood by the great mass of mankind, our moral concerns are firmly grounded in reality:

> Nothing can be more real, or concern us more, than our own sentiments of pleasure and uneasiness; and if these be favourable to virtue, and unfavourable to vice, no more can be requisite to the regulation of our conduct and behaviour. (p. 469)

XI

CONCLUSION

The central theme of this work is that Hume's naturalism and skepticism are mutually supportive. The skepticism I have in mind is not, of course, a moderate, Academic, probabilistic (milk and water) skepticism. An alliance between probabilism and naturalism needs no special explanation. My claim is that an unmitigated epistemological skepticism which, as I have argued, characterizes Hume's philosophy, coheres with Hume's naturalistic program.

A fundamental objection to this claim is that Hume's skepticism (which is an *a priori* philosophical matter) has nothing to do with his naturalistic program (which, rightly understood, involves an *empirical* inquiry into the causes of mental phenomena). To confound the two is to miscast philosophical issues as matters of empirical psychology. This is the charge of psychologism, and here I wish to say something in response to it.[1]

It would be an exaggeration to say that Hume was always careful to distinguish between logical and psychological questions, but his general program not only recognizes this distinction, but depends upon it. Hume's skeptical arguments are intended to show that the logical (or epistemological) issues that philosophers have discussed admit of no solution. He can then turn, with perfect justification, to the factual question of how humans are able to form beliefs despite the skeptical arguments that can be brought against them.

At this point, however, Hume's critics may claim that Hume is no longer doing philosophy and the task of assessing his contribu-

Conclusion

tions can be left to others. This segregationist attitude no longer goes unchallenged. First of all, it is not obvious that we can draw a sharp distinction between logical and psychological considerations or, more generally, between conceptual and non-conceptual issues. The concepts we have are grounded in the kind of creatures we are, in the kinds of practices we engage in, and in the kind of conditioning and training we undergo. This is a sermon preached in one way by Wittgenstein and in another, remarkably Humean, way by Quine. For Quine, the epistemologist has two tasks, one conceptual, the other doctrinal:

> The conceptual studies are concerned with meaning, the doctrinal with truth. The conceptual studies are concerned with clarifying concepts by defining them, some in terms of others. The doctrinal studies are concerned with establishing laws by proving them, some on the basis of others.[2]

More specifically, the task of an epistemology, conceived along empiricist lines, is to show how natural knowledge is based on sense experience.

> This means explaining the notion of body in sensory terms; here is the conceptual side. And it means justifying our knowledge of truths of nature in sensory terms; here is the doctrinal side of the bifurcation.[3]

With respect to the doctrinal question, the question of justifying empirical knowledge, Quine simply embraces Hume's skeptical position: "On the doctrinal side, I do not see that we are farther along today than where Hume left us. The Humean predicament is the human predicament."[4] At this point, Quine adopts precisely the strategy that I have attributed to Hume. With the justificatory issue set aside as unanswerable, it is now unobjectionable to turn to psychology for aid in pursuing *conceptual* issues. Quine makes the point this way:

> If the epistemologist's goal is validation of the grounds of empirical science, he defeats his purpose by using psychology or other empirical science in the validation. However, such scruples against circularity have little point once we have stopped dreaming of deducing science from observations. If

Conclusion

we are out simply to understand the link between observation and science, we are well advised to use any available information, including that provided by the very science whose link with observation we are seeking to understand.[5]

It is important not to exaggerate similarities: Quine considers Hume the paradigm of a philosopher committed to what he dismissively calls the *two dogmas of empiricism*.[6] Still, the manner in which a skepticism with respect to doctrinal (justificatory) questions defuses the charge of psychologism with respect to conceptual issues is remarkably similar. Once a radical skepticism destroys foundationalist dreams, the charge of psychologism loses its force.

There are, however, other, much simpler, reasons for thinking that skepticism and naturalism cannot lie down peacefully together. Troubles seem to arise from two directions. First, a radical skepticism seems to undercut a naturalistic program, for, given the fact that no causal inference is rationally grounded, what is the point of giving causal explanations of the operations of the human mind? (Given Hume's skepticism with regard to reason, what is the point of engaging in any rational activity at all?) Second, Hume's naturalism seems to undercut his skepticism. If beliefs are the causal products of non-rational processes, what is the point of making epistemic assessments, be they skeptical or not?

To answer these questions, we must recognize the central importance of Hume's idea that philosophical positions, including his own, are the product of causal factors. As we saw in Chapter VII, philosophical reflection follows a determinate course governed by the principles of the human mind. At each stage in our reflections we are naturally inclined to accept certain philosophical positions and, from that perspective, criticize the philosophical views of others.

The point I am making has been insisted upon by Richard Popkin. The ancient skeptics did not recommend silence, instead, they recommended that we report (without dogmatizing) how things naturally strike us. But Hume saw what the ancient skeptics did not see: under certain circumstances philosophizing is itself natural. Popkin characterizes this aspect of Hume's skepticism in these words:

Conclusion

He believes whatever nature leads him to believe, no more and no less. He is compelled to believe, and in accepting the compulsion he is exhibiting his scepticism. He is led to philosophize by certain natural inclinations, and through them to come to certain conclusions, and in so doing he is again exhibiting his scepticism.[7]

The Humean skeptic philosophizes because under certain conditions he is compelled to do so.

The reverse problem, the seeming tendency of Hume's naturalism to undercut all epistemic assessments, hence his skepticism as well, admits of a similar rejoinder. In the *Treatise* Hume constantly furthers certain philosophical views while criticizing others, yet, on his own account, all these views are natural products of the mind's operations. Why should one natural belief be given higher or lower epistemic marks than another? The answer is that the activity of criticism is itself natural. As we reflect upon a given philosophical position, say the theory of double existence, it may strike us as faulty. If so, there is no reason why we (as skeptics) should not say so, thereby giving expression (undogmatically) to the way things strike us from the perspective we occupy at the moment. Hume concludes Book I of the *Treatise* making precisely this point:

> Nor is it only proper we shou'd in general indulge our inclination in the most elaborate philosophical researches, notwithstanding our sceptical principles, but also that we shou'd yield to that propensity, which inclines us to be positive and certain in *particular points*, according to the light, in which we survey them in any *particular instant*. (The emphasis is Hume's, p. 273)

Hume's only worry is that these confident statements made from a particular standpoint will be taken in an unrestricted, hence dogmatic, way. Hume ends Book I asking his reader not to take his pronouncements, however unqualified, as the expression of a dogmatic commitment.

In conclusion, what kind of skepticism shall we attribute to David Hume? Presumably, in daily life he was hardly a skeptic at all: "I find myself absolutely and necessarily determin'd to live, and talk, and act like other people in the common affairs of life"

Conclusion

(p. 269). In certain rare moments of intense reflection he finds himself led into Pyrrhonism:

> The *intense* view of these manifold contradictions and imperfections in human reason has so wrought upon me, and heated my brain, that I am ready to reject all belief and reasoning, and can look upon no opinion even as more probable or likely than another. (pp. 268–9)

Yet Hume constantly recommends a moderate or mitigated skepticism and it is from this standpoint that he normally addresses his reader. How does one attain this state? In the *Enquiry* Hume tells us that this can be brought about by reflection on Pyrrhonian arguments:

> To bring us to so salutary a determination, nothing can be more serviceable, than to be once thoroughly convinced of the force of the Pyrrhonian doubt, and of the impossibility, that anything, but the strong power of natural instinct, could free us from it. (p. 162)

For Hume there are no arguments that will refute Pyrrhonism, and that entails that there can be no arguments justifying a more mitigated version of skepticism. The mitigated skepticism that Hume recommends is the causal product of two competing influences: Pyrrhonian doubt on one side, natural instinct on the other. We do not argue for mitigated skepticism; we find ourselves there. In this way Hume's skepticism and naturalism meet in a causal theory of skepticism itself.[8]

In a great many passages Hume asks whether, given his theory of belief, his own theory is likely to be accepted. This is the central question of the opening section of his first *Enquiry* where he contrasts popular philosophy with abstruse philosophy and ruefully wonders whether his own abstruse philosophy would have any deep, lasting, and important effect. These reflections are more than expressions of his disappointment, for passages of the same kind occur throughout the *Treatise*. Thus at the beginning of Book III he tells his reader that the liveliness of the subject may aid the reception of his discussion of morality. "Without this advantage," he says, "I never should have ventur'd upon a third volume of such abstruse philosophy, in an age, wherein the greatest part of

Conclusion

men seem agreed to convert reading into an amusement, and to reject every thing that requires any considerable degree of attention to be comprehended" (p. 456). Hume seems never to have appreciated the confirmation his theory received from its poor reception.

Appendix A

INTERPRETATIONS AND CRITICISMS OF HUME'S INDUCTIVE SKEPTICISM

I

In Chapter IV I presented what I called a rough and ready characterization of Hume's skeptical argument concerning induction. Though superficial, the interpretation follows standard lines; even so (or perhaps because of this) many Hume commentators will find this interpretation objectionable. Here I shall defend it in detail.

If we take the *Abstract* (pp. 650–2) as our guide, it is clear that Hume's argument has the following form:

> Level I: "It is not any thing that reason sees in the cause, which makes us *infer* the effect," because "the mind can always *conceive* any effect to follow from any cause, and indeed any event to follow upon another: whatever we *conceive* is possible, at least in a metaphysical sense: but wherever a demonstration takes place, the contrary is impossible, and implies a contradiction," therefore "all reasonings concerning cause and effect, are founded on experience."
>
> Level II, Step I: "{All} reasonings from experience are founded on the supposition, that the course of nature will continue uniformly the same." It is not possible to "*demonstrate*, that the course of nature must continue uniformly the same," for "what is possible can never be demonstrated to be false; and 'tis possible the course of

Hume's Inductive Skepticism

nature may change, since we can conceive of such a change."

Level II, Step II: There are no proofs "by any *probable* arguments, that the future must be conformable to the past," for "all probable arguments are built on the supposition, that there is this conformity betwixt the future and the past, and therefore can never prove it."

Here we are dealing with a two-level argument, where the second level itself divides into two parts. At the first level Hume asks whether it is possible to draw a warranted causal inference antecedent to experience relating the cause to other events. In the absence of such experience, the inference would have to be demonstrative, but this, Hume argues, is not a live option, since we can consistently conceive of any event following any other.

At the second level, Hume considers what change the accumulation of past experience of a constant conjunction will have on the situation. He holds that past experience will be of use in grounding causal inferences only if we assume a conformity betwixt the future and the past. He then argues that this supposition cannot be justified by demonstrative reasoning, since it is conceivable that the future may not resemble the past. (This is just the first level argument repeating itself, since it says no more than this: whatever our past experience, it is always conceivable that any chain of events can be followed by any kind of event.) Hume then completes his argument by maintaining that any probable argument in behalf of this principle will be circular. Since these are the only sorts of arguments there are (i.e., demonstrative and probabilistic), no argument can justify the supposition upon which our causal reasoning relies. I have called this Hume's *no argument argument*.

Although the argument as it appears in the *Appendix* seems straightforward enough, it has been subjected to competing interpretations. The following interpretative principles may help to sort out these variant readings.

(i) For Hume, there are two sorts of arguments: demonstrative and probable.

(ii) For Hume, there are two sorts of inferences, demonstrative inferences which necessitate their conclusions and probable or inductive inferences which probabilize their conclusions.

(iii) Recognizing both kinds of inference, Hume held that the
principle that nature is uniform could not be justified by
an argument using either kind of inference.

These three theses characterize the position that I claim to find in the text.

Two recent writers, Beauchamp and Rosenberg, have (in effect) challenged the third thesis and as a result ascribe a very limited skepticism to Hume.

> Hume repeatedly argues that induction is nondemonstrative; his model of a demonstrative argument is one that proceeds from self-evident *a priori* premises to a conclusion certified by deductive logic. . . . [T]he larger purpose of Hume's treatment of induction is to attack this rationalistic conception of reason.[1]

They then go on to make the stronger claim that this larger purpose is, indeed, "the whole point of his 'critique' of induction."[2] The shudder quotes around the word "critique" indicate their commitment to the position that Hume never so much as attempted a critique of inductive inferences. We might put their point this way: far from being a *deductivist*, as many critics have urged, the central point of Hume's discussion of induction is to refute deductivism.

We can, I think, make short work of this interpretation. Over against it are the specific statements in Hume's argument that I have labelled Level II, Step II. Since Beauchamp and Rosenberg have not chosen to discuss these passages, their interpretation loses by default.

D. C. Stove, and J. L. Mackie follows him in this, has produced an argument with almost the opposite tendency to Beauchamp and Rosenberg. Stove explicitly rejects the second thesis listed above. He holds that although Hume did distinguish between two sorts of arguments, demonstrative and probable, he did not distinguish between two sorts of inferences. Hume, according to Stove, was a deductivist; he held that there is only one sort of good inference, a deductively valid inference, and all other inferences share the same status of being totally bad. Stove and Mackie are, of course, aware of this reference to *probable arguments* in Hume; how can they maintain their deductivist interpre-

Hume's Inductive Skepticism

tation in the face of them? Part of their argument is an attempt to defuse the reference to probable arguments by claiming that Hume understood the contrast between probable arguments and demonstrative arguments in a different way from us now.

> Our distinction between demonstrative and probable arguments is concerned with their degree of conclusiveness, not with the epistemological character of their premises; it may be called a formal or evaluative distinction. Hume's distinction is a material or descriptive one, concerned solely with the epistemological character of the premises.[3]

On this reading, the distinctive mark of a deductive argument is that it puts forth necessary truths in its premises in order to establish a necessary truth in its conclusion. A probable argument is an attempt to establish a contingent conclusion on the basis of contingent premises. Thus if Stove is right, far from refuting the claim that there can be no inductive (probabilizing) support for the principle of uniformity, Hume never so much as considered this possibility.

I don't think that the text of the *Treatise* supports this interpretation of Hume's argument. In the first place, Hume's explicit discussions of probability (in Sections xi–xiii, Part III, Book I) can only be read as an attempt to give a psychological explanation of how premises can supply something less than full support to a conclusion. Stove's response is to abuse these parts of the *Treatise*. He first claims that they are not essential to understanding Hume's philosophy of inductive inference, citing as evidence the fact that this part of the *Treatise* is not mentioned in the *Abstract*.[4] He then goes on to bludgeon the text:

> But sections xi–xiii are not only an inessential part of Hume's philosophy of induction. They are, philosophically considered, altogether unrewarding intrinsically.
> Commentators on Hume have without exception failed to extract from them anything of philosophical interest.[5]

Perhaps these sections are as bad as Stove says (I discuss them in some detail in Chapter V), but however this may be, they still show that Hume did not use the term "probable" in the restrictive sense suggested by Stove.

Furthermore, the idea that a set of premises can bestow upon its conclusion a degree of probability between 0 and 1 is an essential assumption in his skepticism with regard to reason, where, as we have seen, Hume argues that successive evaluations will successively diminish the degree of probability "to nothing." Recognizing a threat from this direction, Stove again gives the text a thumping:

> The argument of that section need not be expounded here. It is, and has been generally recognized as being, not merely defective, but one of the worst arguments ever to impose itself on a man of genius.[6]

Perhaps Stove is right in this assessment of Hume's argument, but this in no way blunts the charge that Stove is simply wrong in his interpretation of what Hume meant by probable arguments.

I don't think that Stove's textual arguments carry much force, but his reconstructive arguments are much stronger and are at least arguably correct. Stove maintains that Hume's arguments make sense only if we attribute the deductivist thesis to him. The central issue here turns upon the proper interpretation of the charge of circularity that is made against the use of probable arguments to establish the supposition of a conformity betwixt the future and the past. Stove makes a plausible suggestion that provides the basis for his deductivist interpretation (and later his anti-deductivist criticism) of Hume's argument. Using his word "presupposition" for Hume's "supposition," he makes the following interpretative claim:

> Sometimes when we say of an argument for p to q, that it presupposes r, our meaning is as follows: that, as it stands, the argument from p to q is not valid, and that, in order to turn it into a valid argument, it would be necessary to add to its premises the proposition r. I believe that this is the sense in which "presuppose" occurs in the premise[s] of Hume's argument.[7]

So even without his thesis that Hume used the notions of demonstrative and probable in a way different from the way that we do, Stove could still insist that Hume was, after all, a deductivist, for when he turns to the examination of inductive arguments, he assumes, as a matter of course, that they are no good if they do not meet the standards of a valid deductive argument.

Hume's Inductive Skepticism

My own opinion is that this issue cannot be resolved because Hume's text is underdetermined on this matter, but I think that Stroud provides an explanation of Hume's argument that both squares with the text and avoids the charge of deductivism. According to Stroud, Hume asks, quite generally, whether it is *reasonable* for us to believe that past regularities should be projected into the future. Now in Stroud's words:

> By concentrating on this aspect of reasonableness Hume could find support for his claim that a reasonable belief in something unobserved requires more than certain kinds of past and present experiences. It requires as well that one reasonably believe that what one has experienced is good reason to believe what one does about the unobserved. And then Hume's question, which he thinks leads to scepticism, is how one can ever get a reasonable belief to that effect.
>
> If that question does in fact lead to scepticism, it is not because Hume implicitly assumes that all reasons must be deductively sufficient.[8]

I think that Stroud's point can be made without using the term "reasonable" and thereby stirring old Oxbridge complaints. The point is that the charge that someone is supposing the very matter at issue does not, *eo ipso*, commit the person making the charge to deductivism. Perhaps an analogy will help bring out the force of Stroud's response. We can imagine a legislature that is deeply distrusted by its people. In response, the legislature undertakes an investigation and declares itself trustworthy. Clearly, the people will not be satisfied with these assurances, since the inquiry is subject to the same doubts that initiated it. It is, I think, in this sense that Hume holds that probable arguments in support of the claim that nature is uniform suppose the very thing at issue. Looked at this way, it is hard to see how deductivism comes in at all.

II

Responses to Hume's inductive skepticism fall into two main categories: (1) those that accept Hume's challenge as legitimate and attempt to meet it by producing a justificatory argument on behalf of induction, and (2) those that argue that Hume's challenge is improper or anyway unimportant.

(1) The most plausible attempts to *justify* induction fall into two groups: inductive justifications and pragmatic justifications. Taking the first route, John Stuart Mill agreed with Hume that all inductive inferences rely upon the principle that nature is uniform, but then argued, denying the charge of circularity, that we have good (and growing) inductive evidence for holding that nature *is* uniform. In particular, our scientific success in finding specific regularities gives us good grounds by enumerative induction for holding that nature as a whole is uniform.[9] Now put this way, Mill seems only to have thrown himself on the sword of Hume's argument, for Hume could reply that even if *all* events in the past have been instances of perfect regularity, we may still ask by what right we project these regularities into the future.

Yet Mill's argument has a point. If our persistent efforts never turned up uniformities in nature, then, supposing that we could survive, this would give us some (though not conclusive) evidence for holding that nature is *not* uniform. Thus an inductive justification of the principle that nature is uniform seems to be carried on at risk. Working on the assumption that nature is uniform, we might carry out investigations that tended to show that this assumption is false.

More recent inductive attempts to justify induction transform Mill's argument in the following way: they speak of an inductive justification of our inductive *procedures* rather than a justification of the claim that nature is uniform.[10] We could, for example, make an inductive investigation of the comparative success of inductive procedures over other methods for forecasting the future, say wishful thinking and random guessing. Again, although the procedure is itself inductive, it is carried on with the risk that inductive reasoning may not prove superior to these other methods. To borrow a phrase from Brian Skyrms, our inductive procedures may not be "inductively coherent with the facts."[11] So even if using inductive procedures to justify induction may in some way (or at some level) be circular, it is not a procedure that guarantees its own success. In fact we do have good inductive evidence for holding that the procedures of scientific induction are superior to wishful thinking and random guessing. In this sense it is not only possible to provide an inductive justification

Hume's Inductive Skepticism

for inductive procedures, we have actually come a considerable distance in doing so.

I do not think that Hume would disagree with these last remarks, indeed, I think that he would give them his wholehearted support. He was, after all, a propagandist for the inductive methods of empirical science.[12] None of this, however, is responsive to Hume's skeptical challenge to induction. Hume was not presenting a weight of evidence argument, i.e., he was not arguing from within the framework of inductive reasoning that the procedures of induction are no better than any other method of drawing inferences beyond experience. His challenge was global; he was querying the credentials of the entire inductive enterprise. In sum, the response made to Mill can now be repeated, only at a higher level: even if we grant that inductive procedures have uniformly done a better job of producing good predictions than any other procedure, we still want to know by what right we project this uniformity (of good predicting) into the future.

The essence of pragmatic justifications is to argue that employing the methods of scientific induction is the best strategy open to us – or at least no worse than any other. I shall not go into any of this in detail, for the arguments here are often technical and complex,[13] yet as far as I can see, none of these pragmatic justifications goes beyond (or can go beyond) the ordinal claim that inductive methods are better than (or at least no worse than) other methods for inferences beyond experience. Since this is compatible with the claim that no method of prediction provides *significant* grounds for assent, this seems to sidestep Hume's challenge rather than meet it. Since I shall make a similar response to D. C. Stove's criticisms of Hume's inductive skepticism, I shall postpone comments on this matter till then.

(2) Dismissive attacks upon Hume's skeptical arguments have been popular for the last two or three decades, but, as far as I can see, they either misrepresent Hume's position or, without realizing it, answer Hume's skepticism in a way that does not mitigate it. Two popular responses fall into the misrepresentation camp. To see this, we have to keep in mind that Hume was concerned with *arguments*. He maintained, first, that all inferences that take us from experience beyond experience rely on the principle that nature is uniform. He maintained further that no argument of any kind can establish that nature is uniform, for

Hume's Inductive Skepticism

arguments come in only two kinds, deductive and inductive, and neither kind of argument can establish this principle. His conclusion, then, is that no argument can establish the credentials of our inductive inferences. I have called this Hume's No-Argument Argument.

A common linguistic response to Hume's inductive skepticism goes something like this: predicting future events on the basis of the observation of past regularities, especially when these observations are extensive and cover a wide variety of circumstances, is what *counts* as being reasonable in this domain. The question, then, whether it is reasonable to draw inferences in this way has an affirmative answer backed by an analytic truth. To deny that such inferences are reasonable would, therefore, amount to denying an analytic truth.[14] For all I know, this claim about the word "reasonable" and its cognates is true: we call inferences reasonable if they conform, for example, to standard canons of inductive logic. We could make much the same point by saying that the word "reasonable" is a term of assessment internal to our argumentative procedures, whether they are inductive or deductive. It is thus improper – a misuse of language – to ask whether these argumentative procedures are reasonable or unreasonable at large. By calling these general procedures into question, the background needed for the use of terms of argumentative assessment has been displaced, and these terms lose their function.

As an account of the ordinary use of such words as "reasonable," "justified," etc., these remarks may be right; thus if Hume says or suggests that all of our inductive procedures are unreasonable, he can be accused of speaking misleadingly or inappropriately. Yet it is hard to see how any of this is responsive to the central claims of Hume's No-Argument Argument: (1) all inductive inferences rely upon the principle that nature is uniform; (2) no argument, either deductive or inductive, can establish this principle; (3) therefore no argument can justify our reliance on inductive inferences. If at this point a critic replies that Hume's argument gains all of its interest from the apparent assertion of the *un*reasonableness of inductive inferences, we might even grant this and merely note that the argument has still remained untouched.[15]

Another common criticism of Hume's argument which strikes

Hume's Inductive Skepticism

me as wrong is that Hume is a deductivist, and his entire argument proceeds from the false assumption that the only good argument is a good deductive argument. As indicated above, I follow Stroud in thinking that the charge of deductivism cannot be shown to hold against Hume. Even so, it is not a wholly implausible reading of the text, and is therefore worth examining in detail. Granting for the moment that Hume's inductive skepticism does involve a commitment to deductivism, I shall argue that this criticism carries much less weight than commonly assumed.

Although Hume has often been accused of being a deductivist, as far as I know, D. C. Stove is the first philosopher to articulate this charge in a rigorous way and then go on to indicate just what is wrong with deductivism. Stove characterizes Hume's inductive skepticism by the following principle:

If e and h are such that the inference from e to h is inductive, $P(h,e.t) = P(h,t)$.[16]

Informally, Hume's inductive skepticism is equivalent to the claim that adding a piece of evidence e to a tautological premise does not increase the inductive support for the conclusion beyond the support already given by the tautology alone. (Thus additional premises will never increase inductive support for the conclusion beyond its initial probability.) Stove characterizes the weaker thesis of inductive fallibilism by the following principle:

If e_1 and h are such that the inference from e_1 to h is inductive, $P(h,e_1.t) < 1$; and if e_2 is observational, $P(h,e_1.e_2.t) < 1$.[17]

Informally, inductive fallibilism amounts to the claim that additional evidence in an inductive argument can never make the conclusion certain. Additional evidence can, however, raise the support for the conclusion above its initial probability (i.e., the degree of support given it by a tautology).

Stove's central claim, and this has been made by many others as well, is that Hume's argument for inductive skepticism as opposed to inductive fallibilism depends upon a commitment to *deductivism*. Informally, this is the thesis that the premises of a

Hume's Inductive Skepticism

deductively invalid argument lend no support whatsoever to the conclusion of such an argument. More carefully, the premises of a deductively invalid argument lend no more support to the conclusion than a tautology would. This is expressed by the following principle:

If e and h are such that e does not entail h, $P(h,e.t) = P(h,t)$.[18]

Now others have attacked Hume for accepting this deductivist thesis; it amounts, as it is often said, to recognizing only one kind of argument, and rejecting inductive arguments simply because they are not deductive. This is sometimes called *deductive chauvinism*. Stove's argument goes beyond this general charge in maintaining that the thesis of deductivism is actually inconsistent with a combination of standard *principles* of probability, that are not normally challenged, and certain *statements* of probability, which most people (including Hume) would accept. The four principles of probability are as follows:

(P1) The conjunction principle, $P(q.r,p) = P(q,p) \times P(r,p.q)$.
(P2) The negation principle, $P(q,p) = 1 - P(\sim q.p)$.
(P3) The equivalence principle (that logically equivalent propositions can be substituted for one another *salve probabilitate* in statements and in principles of logical probability).
(P4) The lower limit principle, $P(q,p) > = 0$.

The two statements of probability take the following form:

(S1) $P(\sim Fb \vee \sim Fa, t) < 1$
(S2) $P(Fa,t) < 1$.[19]

Here "F" is an observational predicate. The intuitive idea behind these two statements is that the initial probability of an observation statement is always less than 1. From these six premises, Stove uses an argument that he attributes to von Thum to derive the further statement of probability:

(S3) $P(Fb.Fa,Fa.t) > P(Fb.Fa,t)$.[20]

Hume's Inductive Skepticism

But this result is incompatible with the thesis of inductive skepticism which entails:

$P(Fb.Fa,Fa.t) = P(Fb.Fa,t)$.

This incompatibility does not establish the falsehood of the thesis of deductivism, for it is possible to challenge one of the six explicit premises of Stove's argument. But if we accept these six premises and the obviously valid deduction from them, the thesis of deductivism is then shown to be false.

There are three options for the defender of Hume. First, he can deny that Hume accepted the thesis of deductivism and thereby block the argument to inconsistency presented by Stove. This is the position I share with Stroud. Alternatively, he can grant that Hume was a deductivist in Stove's sense, and then try to find some good reason for rejecting one of the six premises of Stove's argument. I don't think that the second alternative holds out much promise. The third alternative is a fall-back position. It grants that Stove's refutation of Hume's inductive skepticism is correct, but then suggests that the result of this refutation is much more modest than Stove acknowledges. The difference between inductive skepticism (which according to Stove Hume held and shouldn't) and inductive fallibilism (which according to Stove Hume should have been content with but wasn't) comes to this: there are arguments intermediate between those that give full support and those that give no support to their conclusions. Denying this claim will entail the falsehood of what Stove calls the fundamental thesis of the theory of logical probability: "the fundamental thesis of the theory of logical probability ... is that two arguments may be of unequal degree of conclusiveness, even though both are invalid."[21] But what does this difference come to? A reference to fallibilism suggests an academic brand of skepticism where certainty is eschewed but reason is adjusted to probabilities. But to be a fallibilist in this (traditional) sense presupposes that we can attain some tolerably high degree of inductive support for our conclusion and nothing in Stove's argument has any tendency to guarantee this. It may be true, as Stove has argued, that we can be assured that there are inductive arguments whose premises supply greater inductive support than a tautology would, but there are no grounds, as far as his arguments go, to suppose that this increase is greater than some finite value, however small that finite value might be.

Here we can introduce a new position called ultra-fallibilism. While conceding that inductive skepticism (in Stove's sense) is unfounded, it challenges the standard fallibilist to produce grounds for supposing that the inductive support for any conclusion given by a premise of the form $h.t$ is greater than the inductive support given by t alone *by at least some specifiable amount*. In order to generate specific probability values (other than 1 and 0), principles of probability have to be relativized to some particular language. Given such a relativization, we might then arbitrarily assign initial probabilities to state descriptions or structures on state description. Of course, such arbitrary assignments would not serve our present purposes. Alternatively, we might find some non-arbitrary *empirical* method for assigning initial probabilities to state descriptions or structures on them. I shall not assert dogmatically that this cannot be done without raising anew Hume's skeptical (or at least ultra-fallibilist) doubts concerning induction, but we at least have a right to maintain our suspicions.

The upshot of Stove's criticism seems to be this: inductive skepticism and inductive fallibilism are formally distinct, but until we are given some reason, that is not itself subject to Humean attack, to believe that the inductive fallibilist can establish some determinate degree of inductive support for his conclusions, we have no warrant to maintain a position any stronger than ultra-fallibilism. Needless to say, ultra-fallibilism is a version of Pyrrhonian skepticism rather than moderate skepticism.

Very briefly let me respond to an ingenious criticism of Hume's skeptical argument that has recently been presented by Robert Nozick in his *Philosophical Explanations*. Nozick pictures the skeptic arguing as follows: in order to know that a certain event will occur in the future, I must know that the future will resemble the past, but I cannot know this, therefore, I can never know that a future event will occur. Nozick's response is that my knowledge of this future event does not depend upon having knowledge that the future will resemble the past. According to Nozick, in order

Hume's Inductive Skepticism

for a person S to know something, four conditions must be satisfied.

(1) p is true.
(2) S believes that p.
(3) not-p → not-(S believes that p).
(4) p → S believes that p.

Here (3) and (4) express subjunctive conditionals and the four conditions taken together come to this: "A person knows that p when he not only does truly believe it, but also would truly believe it and wouldn't falsely believe it."[22] When a person's belief meets these conditions, Nozick says that it "*tracks* the truth."[23] Clearly, it is not a necessary condition for a person's belief in a future event to track the truth that he have a further belief that nature is uniform that also tracks the truth. Hence, a person can know that a future event will occur without at the same time knowing that nature is uniform.

I have suggested elsewhere that Nozick's account of knowledge is hardly persuasive and that, anyway, if this is what knowledge amounts to, no skeptic need deny its existence. Hume has produced a no-argument argument to the effect that nothing can justify our reliance on inductive inferences because no argument can justify the principle of the uniformity of nature upon which they rely. Perhaps something can be said in response to this skeptical argument, but Nozick's reflections do not seem to bear upon it. If our world is orderly and our projective mechanisms are well tuned to this orderliness, then our projections will often track the truth. Such projections will constitute Nozick-knowledge. But a person can Nozick-know that p without having the justified belief that p, and therefore Nozick-knowledge is compatible with the soundness of Hume's argument for inductive skepticism and cannot refute it. At most, Nozick can issue only a small complaint against the skeptic. If the skeptic goes on to say that his argument shows that we do not (or cannot) know certain things and if Nozick's account of knowledge is essentially correct, then the skeptic can be accused of *speaking* incorrectly. The skeptic should have been content with saying that certain fundamental principles are incapable of justification but should not have gone on to say that they therefore cannot be known to be true.[24]

Appendix B

HUME'S REGULARITY DEFINITION OF CAUSATION

Criticisms of Hume's first definition of causality come in two main forms: (1) cases where a causal relation seems to exist, but the required regularity is seemingly absent and (2) cases where regularity is present but a causal relation seems to be missing.[1]

I shall not discuss the first kind of counter-example in detail, because I think it has been dealt with adequately by others. So briefly, how could a modern defender of Hume respond to the claim that a short circuit can cause a fire without it being the case that short circuits always cause fires? The simple response is that Hume's regularity theory does not entail that if one short circuit causes a fire then all of them must. The definition makes quite another demand: if this short circuit caused a fire then anything resembling it must produce a fire as well. The crucial point is that Hume's definition does not imply that being a short circuit constitutes an adequate degree of resemblance.

This point can be made more perspicuous by borrowing some ideas from Donald Davidson.[2] In the singular causal judgment "A short circuit caused the fire," we have used certain predicates to describe or, better, to pick out a cause and an effect. We might have used different predicates to pick out these causal relata, and in some cases the picking out can be done without the use of explicit predicates at all, as in "This caused that." There is, then, no reason to assume that the predicates used in referring to causal relata also determine the relevant set of resembling cases. The short circuit counter-example and the endless variations on it depend on this assumption.

Hume's Regularity Definition of Causation

Turning to the second kind of criticism, Reid, it seems, was the first to point out that regularities can exist that are not causal. Reid first describes Hume's position in the following words:

> I know of no author before Mr. Hume, who maintained, that we have no other notion of a cause, but that it is something prior to the effect, which has been found by experience to be constantly followed by the effect.[3]

Given this description of Hume's position, he goes on to say:

> It follows from this definition of cause, that night is the cause of day, and day the cause of night. For no two things have more constantly followed each other since the beginning of the world.[4]

Reid's original objection admits of endless variation. It has been noted, for example, that the rising of the sun is uniformly preceded by the crowing of cocks, yet no one believes that the cock's crowing causes the sun to rise. Furthermore, we sometimes come upon a regularity, perhaps in economics, and then go on to ask whether it is causal, yet if Hume's analysis is correct, there should be no such further question to ask.

The first person, and for rather a long time the only person, to offer a reasonable response to Reid's criticism was the later Scottish commonsense philosopher Thomas Brown. Brown rejected Hume's empiricism and his theory of belief, but he accepted a modified version of Hume's regularity theory of causation. While agreeing with Hume that like causes must always give rise to like effects, he rejected the converse claim that like effects must always arise from like causes. Given this modification, he then went on to offer a straightforward regularity definition of causation. Since Reid's criticism of Hume thus applied to him as well, he was forced to respond to it. This is what he said:

> That darkness and light mutually produce each other, they [i.e., common people] do not believe: and if they did believe it, their belief, instead of confirming the truth of Mr. Hume's theory, would prove it to be false; since it would prove the relation of Cause and Effect to be supposed where there is no customary connection. How often, during a long sleepless

night, does the sensation of darkness – exist, without being followed by the sensation of light?[5]

Notice the absolutely simple point that Brown is making: (dropping the reference to sensations), night is a period of darkness, and we are all familiar with other periods of darkness that are not followed by periods of light. Thus, even if night and day are constantly conjoined, it is not true, as Hume's definition requires, that all those things resembling day are constantly conjoined with those things resembling night.

In sum, Reid has misrepresented Hume's position, for Hume does not say that wherever As and Bs are uniformly related under the relations of contiguity and priority, then a causal relation obtains between any given A and its respective B. His definition has an altogether different logical form which implies the more restrictive claim that if a given A and B stand in the required spatio-temporal relations to one another, and, furthermore, if all those things resembling A stand in the required relationship (pairwise) to those things resembling B, then A is the cause of B. Thus even if we succeed in finding predicates A and B such that all the items picked out by A stand in the demanded spatio-temporal relations to the items picked out by B, this does not show, on Hume's definition, that all those items paired under the spatio-temporal relation are thereby causally related. Again borrowing Davidson's idea, the predicates that we use to pick out events in a regularity do not *eo ipso* determine the resemblance classes appropriate for causal ascription.

Although Brown's response to Reid (and this modern restatement of it) seems to me to be perfectly adequate, it may only be a stopgap, for calling our attention to the reference to resemblance, it invites criticisms at a deeper level. Brown's response turns upon the claim that we have no right to restrict the reference to things similar to nights and days merely to nights and days. How, then, are these resemblance classes determined? To see the logical character of this problem, we can consider two limiting cases: at one extreme, we can lay down the rule that only *numerical identity* constitutes a sufficient degree of resemblance to count as a like case. With this stipulation, there are no *other* like cases to be considered, and we arrive at the result that any event contiguous and prior to another is its cause. This, in fact, is a claim explicitly rejected by Hume (p. 77). At the other extreme, we might consider any degree of resemblance, however remote, sufficient to count as a like case. It is easy to see that under this stipulation concerning resemblance classes all of the causal judgments of science and daily life would be false.

It seems, then, that the plausibility of Hume's first definition turns upon the possibility of giving an adequate specification of resemblance classes, and we can hardly say that we have defended it until this is done. As far as I know, this is not a question that Hume ever raises explicitly. Furthermore, given Nelson Goodman's *new riddle of induction*,[6] we are now sensibly aware of the intractability of this problem. Confronted with the problem of specifying what kinds of resemblances count (which ones are projectable), Hume would probably say that it is a fact of human nature (perhaps modified by custom and habit) that we project certain features, but not others. This is not Hume's answer – he doesn't have one – but it is a thoroughly Humean answer.[7]

A consideration of the Reid counter-example leads naturally to another objection to Hume's definition that has become fashionable in recent years. It is maintained that for Hume a causal law is nothing more than a universal regularity. But this cannot be correct for, so it is argued, causal laws support contrary to fact conditionals, but many regularities, in particular accidental regularities (even if exceptionless) do not. Hume, or the modern defender of Hume, is then challenged to explain, on his definition of causation, how a causal law can support contrary to fact conditionals.

Here there seem to be a number of options open to the friends of Hume.[8] The general strategy is to deny that *lawlikeness* and the capacity to support subjunctive conditionals depend on the *content* of causal laws. Lawlikeness does not depend upon a reference to natural necessity in this world[9] or structures on possible worlds.[10] Instead, lawlikeness may be a function of our *confidence* that a given regularity will continue to hold.[11] It could also be a function of the systematic importance assigned to a regularity in some theoretical framework.[12] To cite one last possibility, we might follow Wittgenstein's lead and take the appearance of modal terms as the sign that a *rule* is being employed. A regularity statement becomes lawful when we go by it, rely on it, and use it to shape our investigations. Each of these theories would demand a full elaboration before its merits could be assessed, but they each agree, to put it crudely, that nothing in the world distinguishes lawlike from non-lawlike regularities. If we wish to draw this distinction, we must turn to the agents who formulate these regularity statements and employ them in particular ways. This turning to the subject is not only compatible with Hume's treatment of causality, it is characteristic of it as evidenced by the reference to ideas in his second definition of a cause.

NOTES

Introduction

1 Passmore, p. 2.
2 I defend this thesis in detail in Fogelin (5).

I Aspects of Hume's Skepticism

1 Hume captures this style of criticism in the *Dialogues Concerning Natural Religion* by having Cleanthes remark:

> Whether your scepticism be as absolute and sincere as you pretend, we shall learn by and by, when the company breaks up; we shall then see whether you go out at the door or the window, and whether you really doubt if your body has gravity or can be injured by its fall, according to popular opinion derived from our fallacious senses and more fallacious experience. (Hume (5), p. 9)

2 Bayle's arguments and Hume's responses to them are discussed in detail in Chapter III.
3 See, for example, Ayer and Kolakowski.
4 About this passage Ayer remarks: "What is this but a rhetorical version of our own thesis that a sentence which does not express either a formally true proposition or an empirical hypothesis is devoid of literal significance?" (Ayer, p. 54).
5 Hume discusses the plain man's notion of individual substances in Section vi of Part I, Book I. The more skeptical examination of the philosopher's notion of an underlying substance occurs in Sections iii–vi of Part I, Book I.
6 I discuss these matters more carefully in Chapter VII.

II Hume's Skepticism Concerning Reason

1 Passmore gives this argument prominence in his chapter entitled "The

Notes to Pages 13–14

Sceptic" (Passmore, pp. 132–7). He does, however, play down its systematic importance, remarking that "in the *Treatise*, the scepticism which Hume learnt from Bayle simply overlays the positivistic-associationist structure of his original argument" (p. 133). The plain implication of this remark is that Hume's skepticism, though undoubtedly present, is not of central importance to his general philosophical program. It may even be an affectation that Hume later outgrew when "his 'literary' impulses were under better control" (p. 133). The point of the present study is to reject this reading and show that Hume's skepticism is a central feature of his philosophy. Passmore discusses Hume's skepticism and diminishes its significance; other writers, especially in more recent books that are generally sympathetic to Hume's philosophy, ignore it. Penelhum dismisses this portion of the *Treatise* in a footnote: "I omit discussion here of the unappetizing arguments of Section 1 of Part IV of Book I of the *Treatise*, 'Scepticism with Regard to Reason'." He then remarks, quite correctly, that this skeptical argument is not repeated in the *Enquiry* (Penelhum (2), p. 198). Neither Stroud nor Capaldi mention the argument at all. The omission in Capaldi's work is extraordinary given the fact that one of his purposes is to show that Hume is utterly misidentified as a skeptic of anything but the most modest kind. His silence on the most obvious contrary text is mystifying. Of more recent writers, Ian Hacking is almost alone in taking this argument seriously by noticing that a correct criticism of it raises important questions concerning the proper interpretation of probabilities on probabilities. See in particular Hacking (2).

2 The argument from the criterion of truth has the following general form: If a person puts forward a claim on any subject whatsoever, he can be asked if he does so on the basis of a criterion of truth or not. If he says no, then he will be discredited. If he says yes, then the criterion itself will be called forth and subjected to the same questioning. Is it based upon a criterion or not? Attempts to answer this higher order question will lead either to dogmatism, circularity or an infinite regress. If the speaker has no criterion for accepting his criterion, then he accepts it dogmatically and is thus discredited. If he invokes the very criterion he is defending, then he is involved in circular reasoning. If he invokes a new criterion, then the question is renewed and an infinite regress is launched. Many variations on this argument are possible. For example, the person can be asked to produce a reason in behalf of what he says and then be led into the same system of traps.

This pattern of argument was a favorite of the ancient skeptics who could ring endless changes on it. (See for example, Sextus Empiricus, Chapters 3–7.) As we shall see, at bottom, Hume's skepticism with regard to reason is simply another variation on this ancient trope.

Hume was undoubtedly familiar with these Pyrrhonistic arguments *via* Bayle's *Dictionary*. He was also familiar with Bishop Peter Huet's remarkable Pyrrhonistic tract *A Philosophical Treatise Concerning the Weakness of Human Understanding*, which he cites in the *Dialogues*

Notes to Pages 16–22

Concerning Natural Religion (Hume (5), p. 16). Other references to this French connection can be found in Popkin (3).

3 Thomas Reid quite rightly objects to this claim on the following grounds:

Philosophers understand probability as opposed to demonstration; the vulgar as opposed to certainty; but this author understands it as opposed to infallibility, which no man claims. One who believes himself to be fallible, may still hold it to be certain that two and two make four, and that two contradictory propositions cannot both be true. He may believe some thing to be probable only, and other things to be demonstrable, without making any pretense to infallibility (Reid (1), p. 740).

4 Thomas Reid makes this point by comparing Hume's argument with Zeno's paradox concerning the "infinite series of stages of Achilles's journey after the old man" (Reid (1), p. 747). He does not, however, offer any argument showing that Hume's series will converge on a finite limit.

5 In fact, I think that this is the best way of making coherent sense out of Hume's claim that the probability must ultimately be reduced "to nothing." (Hacking associates this approach with Neyman's theory of confidence values (Hacking (2), p. 30)). If, instead, we interpret this to mean that the assigned probability must ultimately reach 0, we get the surprising result that the negation of the original proposition must reach 1. Of course, reasoning in this way will quickly generate a paradox, for we can start over again and reduce the probability of the negated proposition to 0. Perhaps Hume would have enjoyed this ingenious paradox, but I see no hint of it in the text.

6 Hacking analyzes the error in Hume's argument in precisely these terms, calling it "a confusion of levels of probability" (Hacking (2), p. 30). Reid seems to be saying the same thing when he remarks:

The Rectitude of the decision does not depend upon the character of the judge, but upon the nature of the case. From that only, must it be determined whether the decision is just. The circumstances that rendered it suspicious are mere presumptions, which have no force against direct evidence. (Reid (1), p. 746)

7 Passmore sees that Hume is presenting an infinite regress argument. He also thinks that Hume would have done better to limit it to an *ad hominem* attack upon Cartesian or "antecedent" skepticism. In fact, however, Hume's claims for this argument were much wider, indeed, unlimited.

8 Earlier Hume remarks that "sceptical reasonings, were it possible for them to exist, and were they not destroyed by their subtility, wou'd be successively both strong and weak, according to the successive dispositions of the mind" (p. 186). That is, reason might produce a skeptical argument, destroy it by applying it back upon itself, but then, free once more to reason, produce the skeptical argument anew – and so on *ad infinitum*.

Notes to Pages 25–36

9 It is important here to see how his theory of belief functions in this context. The reasoning does not depend upon his phenomenological account of beliefs being forceful and lively perceptions. The central point is that the feature that qualifies a perception as a belief is *causally* determined through a connection with immediate experience. It is this causal thesis, not the phenomenological thesis, that moves the argument along.

III Hume's Answer to Bayle's Skepticism Concerning Extension

1 Hume does not mention Bayle by name in this context; indeed, he is nowhere mentioned in the *Treatise*, but a comparison of texts by Norman Kemp Smith leaves no doubt that Bayle's skeptical arguments concerning extension not only occasioned Hume's concern with this issue but gave his own arguments their shape. See Kemp Smith (2), pp. 284–90 and pp. 325–38.
2 Bayle, p. 359.
3 *Ibid.*, pp. 359–60.
4 *Ibid.*, p. 360.
5 *Ibid.*, p. 362.
6 *Ibid.*, p. 363.
7 *Ibid.*
8 *Ibid.*, p. 366.
9 For a further statement of the weakness of Hume's attack upon infinite divisibility, see Anthony Flew's excellent treatment of this subject in his "Infinite Divisibility in Hume's *Treatise*," reprinted in Livingston and King.
10 Flew remarks that this passage conflicts with Hume's earlier claim: "Now 'tis certain we have an idea of extension; for otherwise why do we talk and reason concerning it?" (*Treatise* p. 32; Livingston and King, p. 262n).
11 This does square, however, with Hume's commitment to extensionless minima as opposed to minimal extensions.
12 See *Treatise*, pp. 44ff., and also the inserts in editions E and F of the first *Enquiry*, p. 158.
13 Some philosophers hold that the idea that something could be both colored and extensionless is not only false but *a priori* false. Notice that Hume would say that something could be colored without even *seeming* to be extended. Indeed, this is crucial for his argument. I find this unintelligible.
14 Charles Hendel makes this point in the third Appendix of the second edition of his *Studies in the Philosophy of David Hume*, pp. 498ff.
15 Kemp Smith (2), p. 287.
16 *Ibid.*, p. 287n.
17 *Ibid.*, p. 288.
18 *Ibid.*
19 Bayle, p. 372.

IV Causality, Necessity, and Induction

1. The distinction between relations of ideas and matters of fact may be implicit in many of the arguments in Book I of the *Treatise*, but it makes its first explicit appearance in Book III, pp. 463ff.
2. Kemp Smith (2), pp. 91–2.
3. Hume contrasts relations that "depend entirely on the ideas" with those which "may be changed without any change in the ideas." We can call the former sort of relation a *dependent* relation. I shall argue that, despite his explicit statement to the contrary, Hume is committed to the doctrine that causal relations are dependent relations.

   We can try to capture the notion of a *dependent* relation by taking over the notion of a supervenient property, extending it to relations and then recasting it for our purposes. The following definition of a dependent relation is modeled on a definition of supervenience offered by Jonathan Dancy:

   To say that a relation R is *dependent* on its relata r_1 and r_2 is to say that if the relata satisfy $N_1, N_2 \ldots N_n$ where $N_1, N_2 \ldots N_n$ is a complete natural description of the relata (including all their natural relations) and r_1 bears R to r_2, then any other pair of relata, r_i and r_j, that similarly satisfy $N_1, N_2 \ldots N_n$ must also be related in the same way by the relation R, and the original relata, r_1 and r_2, cannot change with respect to the relation R without changing in respect to $N_1, N_2 \ldots N_n$.

   So defined, dependence is a very weak notion; for example, any natural relationship that obtains between r_1 and r_2 will trivially count as dependent. We get a stronger notion of a supervenient relation by appending to this definition the phrase: "even though the possession of $N_1, N_2 \ldots N_n$ does not entail that r_1 bears R to r_2" (cf. Dancy, p. 373).

   There are some aggravating problems concerning the correct analysis of supervenience, and these are inherited by my weaker notion of dependence as well. The above definition, for example, turns upon a distinction between natural properties and non-natural properties, and that is a notoriously difficult distinction to draw. Furthermore, without further qualifications, it may turn out that every property (and relation) is supervenient and hence the notion itself becomes trivial. Perhaps these difficulties will lead philosophers to abandon the notion of supervenience as a coherent concept, but I cannot pursue that matter further here.

   I have raised this issue because it is an interesting consequence of Hume's *first* definition of a cause that causal relations are not only dependent on the empirical characteristics of their relata (as he denies), but supervenient on them as well. For a to be the cause of b, a must be contiguous and prior to b, and all like objects must stand in like relations of contiguity and priority to one another. On the natural assumptions about likeness that Hume would presumably make, this guarantees that all these like pairs of events must also stand in causal relations to one another. This shows that under Hume's first definition, causal relations satisfy the first half of the definition of *dependence* given above. Turning to the second half of the definition, it is difficult to think of cases where we could say that a causal relation *ceased* to obtain between two entities except possibly in cases where the cause and effect are simultaneous. We might say that a magnet ceased to hold the metal filings, thus letting them fall. It is easy to see that Hume's first definition requires that in such cases there must be some further difference that accounts in this change in causal relatedness. Therefore Hume's first definition satisfies the second half of our definition of dependence as well. Finally, Hume would also hold that no set of natural properties governing e_1 and e_2 and natural relations between them will ever entail that they are causally related. Thus for Hume, despite his remarks to the contrary, causal relations are dependent upon their relata in the strong sense of being supervenient on them.

4 Actually, Hume does not consider spatial contiguity a necessary condition for a causal relation to exist, for later he will argue that causal relations can obtain between non-spatial entities. See pp. 235ff.
5 I discuss this matter in detail in Chapter VI.
6 Mackie (2), pp. 12–13.
7 *Ibid.*, p. 13.
8 See Appendix B for a discussion of the significance of Reid's supposed counter-example to Hume's first definition of cause.

V Skepticism and the Triumph of the Imagination

1 Support for the first reading comes from the passage just cited where we are told that belief (i.e., vivacity) "alone distinguishes [memory and sense] from imagination" (p. 86). Support, in two directions, for the second reading is given by the following passage:

an idea of the memory, by losing its force and vivacity, may degenerate to such a degree, as to be *taken for* an idea of the imagination; so on the other hand an idea of the imagination may acquire such a force and vivacity, as to *pass for* an idea of the memory. (Emphasis added, p. 86)

Plainly, if vivacity can delude us into confusing imagination with sense memory, then it cannot be definitive of the difference between them. More generally, it is hard to see how Hume can distinguish between sense memory, on the one hand, and imagination, on the other, on purely phenomenalist grounds. Instead, in drawing this distinction, he seems to be taking for granted a straightforward causal theory of perception – a theory, by the way, that his own deeper reflections on the problem of perception undercut (see Chapter VI).

2 The imagination fixes belief in the face of skepticism in two contrasting ways: in the skepticism with regard to reason, the imagination *preserved* (some measure) of belief where reason, left to its own devices, would

Notes to Pages 54–60

have destroyed it entirely; while here the imagination *generates* new beliefs that reason would be impotent to produce.

3 Jonathan Bennett offers a detailed critical examination of Hume's concept-empiricism. See Bennett.

4 Perhaps one reason why this discussion, indeed the entire discussion of probability, has received little attention is that it seems to be a paradigm case of Hume's confounding logical and psychological issues, the so-called sin of psychologizing. Stove makes precisely this charge:

> The most important single reason [that commentators on Hume have without exception failed to extract anything of philosophical interest from sections xi–xiii] is that the kind of interest which Hume displays, in the inferences he is discussing, is an empirical, psychological, rather than a logico-philosophical and evaluative one. . . . There was, of course (though we were not concerned with it), a psychological side to Hume's discussion of the predictive-inductive inference too, but it did not there blot out the philosophical side of his subject. In sections xi–xiii it does. (Stove (2), p. 120)

The point of the present chapter is to show that what Stove calls the psychological *side* of Hume's discussion of both predictive-inductive inferences and probabilistic inferences is the central theme of the text. In the closing chapter I consider force that the charge of psychologizing carries against Hume's skeptical position. I argue that it has none.

5 The most remarkable application of Hume's account of the probability of causes occurs in Book II where he uses it in the analysis of hope and fear. Faced with some dreadful but uncertain prospect, the mind feels grief when it contemplates its occurrence and joy when it contemplates its non-occurrence. As the mind alternates between these two perspectives, the feelings of joy and grief alternate as well, proportioned to the probability of the occurrence or non-occurrence of the dreaded event. But as the mind moves back and forth between these two prospects, the feelings have difficulty keeping up, and as a result the feelings of joy and grief become intermixed in a proportion that reflects the probabilities of the occurrence or non-occurrence of the event. The result of this mixture is a new feeling: fear if the event is likely, hope if it is unlikely.

6 In their essay "Belief in the law of small numbers," Tversky and Kahneman argue that

> people view a sample randomly drawn from a population as highly representative, that is, similar to the population in all essential characteristics. Consequently, they expect any two samples drawn from a particular population to be more similar to one another and to the population than sampling theory predicts, at least for small samples. (Kahneman, Slovic, and Tversky, p. 24)

The similarity between this discussion and Hume's remarks about the influence of general rules is striking. Indeed, there are many close similarities among Hume's treatment of *unphilosophical probability*

Notes to Pages 60–80

and the views collected in Kahneman, Slovic, and Tversky's *Judgments under Uncertainty: Heuristics and Biases*. These writers seem, however, to be unaware of Hume as a predecessor, since he is not mentioned in their long (thirty-page) list of references.

7 Later in the *Treatise* Hume again refers to this *species* of probability associated with general rules: "*General rules* create a species of probability, which sometimes influences the judgment, and always the imagination" (p. 585).

8 For a systematic development of ideas along these lines, see Goldman (2).

VI Skepticism with Regard to the Senses

1 In this chapter I have gone over material that is more than adequately dealt with by others, for example, in Stroud, Passmore, and Penelhum (2). I have also profited from Cook. Perhaps only the discussion of Hume's Berkeleyan problem toward the end of the chapter is original, but this could not be introduced without first sketching the main lines of argument in this section of the *Treatise*.

2 I discuss Hume's criticisms of double existence theories in the next chapter.

3 Price attempts a phenomenalist reconstruction of Hume's position. The central difference between Hume's position and twentieth-century phenomenalism is that Hume is attempting to explain the origin of the plain man's belief in the continued existence of what he sees, whereas twentieth-century phenomenalists are attempting to vindicate it.

4 I'm not sure that Hume is right here. If a pain has a very particular character in virtue of which it can be reidentified as the same again, it does seem natural (however fantastic from a philosophical point of view) to say that *it* has returned.

5 Hume here seems to forget that 0 and 1 are numbers. He probably should have spoken of *plurality* which is the proper contrast to unity.

6 An explanation just like this occurs in Book II, where Hume maintains that hope and fear emerge because of an alternation of the mind between joy and grief (p. 441).

7 It is not obvious what Hume means by an association of dispositions, but if he is thinking of similarities in underlying causal mechanisms rather than similarities in mental contents, his associationist theory will be extended in a fundamental way.

8 These passages occur in sections 3 and 4 of the first part of the *Principles of Human Knowledge*. The argument is repeated throughout the text of Berkeley (1).

9 Berkeley (2), pp. 200–1.

VII Hume's Natural History of Philosophy

1 To the best of my knowledge, no commentator on Hume has given prominence to the idea that philosophical views are themselves the

product of natural causes. In contrast, I think that this provides the key for understanding the character of Hume's skepticism. I shall argue for this thesis in the closing chapter.
2 Bouwsma, p. 3.
3 Wittgenstein, Nos. 398–400.
4 Berkeley (1), p. 45.

VIII The Soul and the Self

1 For a useful summary of the various interpretations of Hume's worries about personal identity, see Don Garrett's "Hume's Self Doubts about Personal Identity," pp. 337-58.
2 At this point Hume pauses to comment on the fact that the plain man, as well as the metaphysician, often fall into the error of assigning a place to things which, properly speaking, can have no place. To illustrate this error, he cites the common belief that the taste of a fig is actually located within the fig. This, Hume thinks, leads to the absurdity of assigning a definite shape to the flavor. Hume seems not to realize that the same absurdity (if it be one) arises when we assign a shape to a hue. By a parity of reasoning, Hume should argue that it is the region with a hue, not the hue itself, that has shape.
3 Hume goes on to remark that this "evidently gives the advantage to the materialist, above their antagonists" (p. 250). Here he seems to forget that the immaterialist also has a problem in explaining causal relationships between material and immaterial objects, e.g., he must explain how an immaterial event (a decision) can bring about a material event (the movement of a limb). Hume's theory thus disembarrasses the immaterialist as well.
4 Hume's understanding of Spinoza plainly relies on Bayle's *Dictionary*.
5 Hume (5), p. 111. Hume was taken with the idea that disputes concerning where to draw a line on a continuum are merely *verbal*. The notion occurs again in an appendix to *An Enquiry Concerning the Principles of Morals* entitled "Of Verbal Disputes."
6 McIntyre, p. 82. McIntyre goes on to suggest that a relatively stable system of overlapping perceptions may provide sufficient continuity for Hume's purposes. This, however, would make perceptions less *fleeting* than Hume seems to treat them in his discussion of the skepticism with regard to the senses.
7 Passmore, pp. 82ff.; D. G. C. MacNabb, pp. 151-2; Wade L. Robison, pp. 181-93.
8 Nelson Pike has responded to interpretations of this kind in his "Hume's Bundle Theory of the Self: A Limited Defense," Pike, pp. 159-65. At the very least, Pike has shown that a response is available which, whether adequate or not, is of a kind that Hume typically accepted. Penelhum (1), pp. 83ff. and Garrett, pp. 343ff. adopt a similar response to this interpretation of Hume's worries.
9 David Pears (1), p. 215.
10 Stroud, p. 126.

11 S. C. Patten presents a similar view in his "Hume's Bundles, Self-Consciousness, and Kant," pp. 59–64.
12 Pears (1), p. 216.
13 Stroud, pp. 138–9.
14 *Ibid.*, p. 140.
15 For an exact statement of this argument, see Garrett, pp. 350–4. A similar line has been adopted by A. H. Basson in his *David Hume*, p. 132.
16 Garrett (1), p. 350.
17 *Ibid.*, p. 352.
18 Hume's uncritical commitment to the way of ideas did not change in his later writings and, for whatever reason, he did not seem disturbed when it was explicitly challenged by Thomas Reid.
19 Penelhum (2), p. 88. This view was first presented by him in his essay "Hume on Personal Identity," Penelhum (1).
20 *Ibid.*, p. 80. In a brief discussion, MacNabb makes essentially the same point. See MacNabb, pp. 147–8.
21 The consequence that, on Hume's theory, a single perception will constitute a minimum bundle, hence a mind, was pointed out to me by Gareth B. Matthews, citing the following passage from the Appendix to the *Treatise* to support this:

> We can conceive a thinking being to have either many or few perceptions. Suppose the mind to be reduc'd even below the life of an oyster. Suppose it to have only one perception, as of thirst or hunger. Consider it in that situation. Do you conceive any thing but merely that perception? Have you any notion of *self* or *substance*? If not, the addition of other perceptions can never give you that notion. (p. 634)

IX Reason and the Passions

1 Ardal's *Passion and Value in Hume's Treatise* remains the standard work on the details of Hume's account of passions.
2 Throughout the discussion, Hume speaks more or less indifferently about the understanding's inability to raise either a passion or give rise to an action. This is because he takes it for granted that a passion can give rise to an action.
3 Hume's references to truth are always obscure and he nowhere goes beyond a naive expression of some kind of correspondence theory. We shall examine another similar passage in Hume's discussion of morality (p. 126).
4 Stroud makes this point (pp. 155ff.).
5 *G & G*, vol. III, p. 197n.
6 *Ibid.*, pp. 45–6.
7 *Ibid.*, p. 47.
8 *Ibid.*
9 *Ibid.*, p. 219n.

10 For the comparison with secondary qualities, see, for example, the *Treatise*, p. 469.
11 *G & G*, vol. III, p. 231.
12 *Ibid.*, p. 219.
13 *Ibid.*, p. 222.
14 *Ibid.*, p. 223.
15 *Ibid.*, p. 224.
16 *Ibid.*
17 *Ibid.*, pp. 226–7.
18 *Ibid.*, p. 228.
19 *Ibid.*, p. 229n.
20 *Ibid.*, pp. 229–30n.
21 *Ibid.*, p. 230n.
22 *Ibid.*

X Reason and Morals

1 For example, Mackie, whose position is basically Humean in many respects, invokes the argument from relativity in Mackie (3), pp. 36–8.
2 *G & G*, vol. III, p. 269.
3 *Ibid.*, p. 99.
4 *Ibid.*, p. 245.
5 In recent years a number of compatibilists (or soft determinists) have defended a position similar to that developed by Hume in Section VIII of the *Enquiry*. (A good bibliography concerning this position can be found in Cornman, Lehrer and Pappas.) The primary emphasis in most modern compatibilist writings is the vindication of freedom. Hume's almost exclusive concern in the *Treatise* and his primary concern in the *Enquiry* was the justification of determinism.
6 *Enquiry*, p. 90.
7 *G & G*, vol. III, pp. 217–18. Hume expressed a similar view in a letter to Francis Hutcheson:

I wish from my heart, I could avoid concluding, that since morality, according to your opinion as well as mine, is determined merely by sentiment, it regards only human nature and human life. . . . If morality were determined by reason, that is the same to all rational creatures: but nothing but experience can assure us, that the sentiments are the same. (Reprinted in Raphael, vol. II, p. 111)

8 *Ibid.*, p. 219n, emphasis added.
9 What I say here is modelled after some remarks made by Jonathan Harrison, pp. 3ff.
10 Sidgwick, p. 384n.
11 Harrison, p. 25. The dreadful quality of this argument leads Harrison, who is usually unflagging in his attempts to give the most sympathetic interpretation of the text, to remark "where this argument is concerned, one almost feels inclined to accept [Hume's] low assessment of the *Treatise*" (pp. 25–6).

12 At this point, Hume could certainly appeal to what Mackie calls the "argument from queerness." Specifically, the intuitionist can be pressed to explain the relationship between an action's moral qualities and these non-moral qualities in virtue of which it possesses its moral qualities. See Mackie (2), pp. 38ff., particularly p. 41, and also Fogelin (1), pp. 175ff.
13 In his elegant essay " 'Was – Must Be' and 'Is – Ought' in Hume," Lewis White Beck examines the parallels between Hume's skeptical arguments concerning induction and his skeptical arguments concerning morality. Except for some differences in emphasis and detail, the present discussion follows Beck's.
14 This point has been made by Barry Stroud. See in particular Stroud, Chapter VIII, "Reason, Passion, and Morality," pp. 171ff.
15 *G & G*, vol. III, p. 267.
16 See Stroud, p. 181 and Harrison, p. 13.
17 Ian Hacking preaches this sermon at large in his book *Why Does Language Matter to Philosophy?*
18 Stroud, pp. 184–5. Similarly, while acknowledging that the text can not fully support this interpretation, Mackie ascribes what he calls an "objectification" theory to Hume, commenting that a "merit of this analysis [of moral judgments], and perhaps a further reason for ascribing it to Hume, is that it is very largely correct" (Mackie (3) p. 72). For more on this issue, and some remarks on differences between Hume's anti-rationalist approach and Mackie's game-theoretic standpoint, see the author's review of Mackie's *Hume's Moral Theory*, Fogelin (4).
19 Mackie, for one, has no difficulties in accepting the global falsehood of moral judgments. He also makes the correct claim that a theory that has this consequence cannot be called skeptical (Mackie (3), p. 35). Here Mackie's claim parallels one I have made about Hume's skepticism with regard to the senses: Hume's theory implies that virtually all of our common perceptual judgments (in ascribing a feature to what we take to be a distinct and continued existence) are false, and that is not a skeptical thesis. Yet, beyond this, Hume is also a skeptic about perception. The plain man's views are false (or at least not true) because they contain a false presupposition. Philosophy removes this false presupposition, but then further reflection leads to the skeptical conclusion that we have no grounds to believe that our perceptions are revelatory of an independent reality. The philosopher can avoid the plain man's false beliefs, but he is not in a position to replace them with anything better. Although the text is not well developed on these matters, it seems clear that Hume is a skeptic in the same way with regard to morals. After the false presupposition of the common man's moral judgments are removed, we still find ourselves completely incapable of justifying or rationally grounding our moral judgments.
20 For a defense of this view with respect to the artificial virtues, see Baron.

XI Conclusion

1. Stove is a recent example of a long line of critics who have deplored Hume's tendency (as they see it) to confuse logical with psychological issues. See Stove (2), pp. 120ff.
2. Quine (2), pp. 69–70.
3. *Ibid.*, p. 71.
4. *Ibid.*, p. 72.
5. *Ibid.*, pp. 75–6.
6. See Quine (1).
7. Popkin (1), p. 95.
8. This paragraph parallels the closing paragraph of Fogelin (5). In that essay I argue that Hume's attitude toward skepticism did not change in a systematic way after the publication of the *Treatise*.

Appendix A Interpretations and Criticisms of Hume's Inductive Skepticism

1. Beauchamp and Rosenberg, p. 43.
2. *Ibid.*
3. Stove (1), p. 198.
4. Stove (2), pp. 119–20.
5. *Ibid.*, p. 120.
6. *Ibid.*, p. 132.
7. *Ibid.*, p. 43.
8. Stroud (1), p. 62.
9. Mill, pp. 184–5 and 337–43.
10. A brief and clear account of various responses to Hume's inductive skepticism can be found in Skyrms (1).
11. *Ibid.*, p. 39.
12. This appears on the title page itself where Hume declares that his work is "An Attempt to introduce the experimental Method of Reasoning INTO MORAL SUBJECTS."
13. Skyrms (1) has a good introductory discussion of the pragmatic justifications of induction of the kind put forward by Reichenbach and Salmon, pp. 41–8.
14. Strawson's discussion in the second part of his final chapter of *Logical Theory* is usually cited as the source of this position, but others have held it as well. See, for example, Edwards (1).
15. To the claim that inductive reasoning is one of our fundamental modes of thinking and therefore beyond proof, it is worth replying that this is something that Hume's no-argument argument (if correct) establishes. In contrast, Hume's dismissive critics assume this dogmatically.
16. Stove (2), p. 61.
17. *Ibid.*
18. *Ibid.*, p. 60.
19. *Ibid.*, pp. 68–9.
20. *Ibid.*, p. 69.

21 *Ibid.*, p. 9.
22 Nozick, p. 178.
23 *Ibid.*
24 These final sentences are taken pretty much *verbatim* from Fogelin (5).

Appendix B Hume's Regularity Definition of Causation

1 Mackie (1) provides a survey of the various counterexamples that have been presented against Hume's regularity definition. See also Mackie (2).
2 Davidson. Beauchamp and Rosenberg rely upon Davidson here as well (Beauchamp and Rosenberg, pp. 93–8).
3 Reid (2), p. 334.
4 *Ibid.*
5 Brown, pp. 170. Brown's full discussion shows genuine sophistication and should be better known.
6 Goodman.
7 The problem of projectable resemblances does appear, at least indirectly, in the *Enquiry* and provides the basis for a skeptical argument that has been ignored by most Hume commentators. Hume entertains the possibility, suggested by the science of his time and completely justified since, that the basic causal regularities are *secret* in the sense of being unobservable. We exist, as he says, in a "natural state of ignorance with regard to the powers and influence of all objects" (*Enquiry*, p. 37). In other words, we have reason to believe that the regularities we project are not fundamental regularities and thus live in the faith that regularities we do project are at least uniform reflections of these underlying regularities. This leads Hume to formulate another version of his skepticism with regard to induction which is, I think, absent from the *Treatise*.

   Let the course of things be allowed hitherto ever so regular; that alone, without some new argument or inference, proves not that, for the future, it will continue so. In vain do you pretend to have learned the nature of bodies from our past experience. Their secret nature, and consequently all their effects and influence, may change, without any change in their sensible qualities. (*Enquiry*, p. 38)

8 In what follows I rely heavily on the excellent discussion in Beauchamp and Rosenberg, pp. 119–70.
9 Kneale.
10 Lewis (1).
11 Ayer (2).
12 Skyrms (2).

BIBLIOGRAPHY

ARDAL, P. S.
Passion and Value in Hume's Treatise, Edinburgh University Press, 1966.
AYER, A. J.
(1) *Language, Truth and Logic*, Dover Publications, New York, n.d.
(2) *Probability and Evidence*, Macmillan, London, 1973.
BARON, Marcia
"Hume's Noble Lie: An Account of His Artificial Virtues," *Canadian Journal of Philosophy*, vol. xii, no. 3, 1982.
BASSON, A. H.
David Hume, Penguin, Baltimore, 1958.
BAYLE, Pierre
Historical and Critical Dictionary, ed. and trans. Richard H. Popkin, The Liberal Arts Press, Indianapolis, 1965.
BEAUCHAMP, T. L., and ROSENBERG, A.
Hume and the Problem of Causation, Oxford University Press, New York, 1981.
BECK, Lewis White
" 'Was–Must–Be' and 'Is–Ought' in Hume," *Philosophical Studies*, vol. 26, 1974.
BENNETT, Jonathan
Locke, Berkeley, Hume, Clarendon, Oxford, 1971.
BERKELEY, George
(1) *Principles of Human Knowledge*, in vol. ii, *The Works of George Berkeley*, edited by A. A. Luce and T. E. Jessop, Thomas Nelson & Sons, London, 1949.
(2) *Three Dialogues between Hylas and Philonous*, in vol. ii, *The Works of George Berkeley*, ed. A. A. Luce and T. E. Jessop, Thomas Nelson & Sons, London, 1949.
BOUWSMA, O. K.
Philosophical Essays, University of Nebraska Press, Lincoln, 1965.

Bibliography

BROWN, Thomas
Cause and Effect, 3rd edn, Mark Newman, Andover, Massachusetts, 1822.

CAPALDI, Nicholas
David Hume, Twayne, Boston, 1975.

CHAPPELL, V. C. (ed.)
Hume, Doubleday, New York, 1966.

CHURCH, Ralph W.
Hume's Theory of the Understanding, Allen & Unwin, London, 1968.

COOK, John W.
"Hume's Scepticism with Regard to the Senses," *American Philosophical Quarterly*, vol. 5, no. 1, 1968.

CORNMAN, James, LEHRER, Keith, and PAPPAS, George
Philosophical Problems and Arguments: An Introduction, 3rd edn, Macmillan, New York, 1982.

DANCY, Jonathan
"On Moral Properties," *Mind*, vol. xc, no. 349, 1981.

DAVIDSON, D.
"Casual Relations," *Journal of Philosophy*, vol. lxiv, 1967.

EDWARDS, Paul
(1) "Bertrand Russell's Doubts About Induction," in *Logic and Language, First Series*, ed. A. Flew, Blackwell, Oxford, 1951.
(2) *Encyclopedia of Philosophy*, 8 vols, ed. P. Edwards, Macmillan and Free Press, New York, 1967.

FLEW, A.
(1) *Hume's Philosophy of Belief*, Routledge & Kegan Paul, London, 1961.
(2) "Infinite Divisibility in Hume's *Treatise*," in Livingston and King (1).

FOGELIN, Robert
(1) *Evidence and Meaning*, Routledge & Kegan Paul, London, 1967.
(2) *Wittgenstein*, Routledge & Kegan Paul, London, 1976.
(3) "Kant and Hume on the Simultaneity of Causes and Effects," *Kant Studien*, vol. 67, no. 4, 1976.
(4) Review: *Hume's Moral Theory*, by J. L. Mackie, *Journal of Philosophy*, vol. LXXIX, no. 4, 1982.
(5) "The Tendency of Hume's Scepticism," *The Sceptical Tradition*, ed. Miles Burnyeat, University of California Press, Berkeley, 1983.
(6) "Hume and the Missing Shade of Blue," forthcoming, *Philosophy and Phenomenological Research*.
(7) Review: *Philosophical Explanations*, by Robert Nozick, forthcoming, *Journal of Philosophy*.

GARRETT, Don
"Hume's Self Doubts about Personal Identity," *The Philosophical Review*, vol. xc, no. 3.

GOLDMAN, Alvin, I.
(1) "Discrimination and Perceptual Knowledge," *The Journal of Philosophy*, vol. 73, 1976.

Bibliography

(2) "Epistemics: The Regulative Theory of Cognition," *The Journal of Philosophy*, vol. 75, 1978.
(3) "Epistemology and the Psychology of Belief," *The Monist*, vol. 61, 1978.
(4) "Varieties of Cognitive Appraisal," *Nous*, vol. 13, 1979.

GOODMAN, Nelson
Fact, Fiction and Forecast, Harvard University Press, Cambridge, Mass., 1955.

HACKING, Ian
(1) *Why Does Language Matter to Philosophy?* Cambridge University Press, 1975.
(2) "Hume's Species of Probability," *Philosophical Studies*, vol. 33, 1978.

HALL, Roland
A Hume Bibliography from 1930, University of York, 1971.

HARRISON, Jonathan
Hume's Moral Epistemology, Clarendon, Oxford, 1976.

HENDEL, Charles W.
Studies in the Philosophy of David Hume, Bobbs-Merrill, Indianapolis, 1963.

HUET, Peter
A Philosophical Treatise Concerning the Weakness of Human Understanding, printed by Gysbert Dommer, London, 1725.

HUME, David
(1) *A Treatise of Human Nature*, ed. L. A. Selby-Bigge, text revised with notes by P. H. Nidditch, Oxford University Press, 1978.
(2) *Enquiries Concerning the Human Understanding and Concerning the Principles of Morals*, ed. L. A. Selby-Bigge, text revised with notes by P. H. Nidditch, Oxford University Press, 1975.
(3) *The Philosophical Works*, 4 vols, ed. T. H. Green and T. H. Grose, London, 1886, reprinted Scientia Verlag Aalen, 1964.
(4) *The Natural History of Religion*, ed. H. E. Root, Stanford University Press, Stanford, Ca., 1967.
(5) *Dialogues Concerning Natural Religion*, ed. with commentary by Nelson Pike, Bobbs-Merrill, Indianapolis, 1970.
(6) *The Letters of David Hume*, 2 vols (ed. J. Y. T. Grieg), Oxford University Press, 1969.
(7) *New Letters of David Hume*, ed. R. Klibansky and E. C. Mossner, Oxford University Press, 1969.

KAHNEMAN, Daniel, SLOVIC, Paul, TVERSKY, Amos (eds)
Judgments under Uncertainty: Heuristics and Biases, Cambridge University Press, 1982.

KANT, Immanuel
Kant's Critique of Pure Reason (trans. Norman Kemp Smith), Macmillan, London, 1953.

KNEALE, W. C.
"Natural Laws and Contrary to Fact Conditionals," in Macdonald, *Philosophy and Analysis*, Philosophical Library, New York, 1954.

Bibliography

KOLAKOWSKI, Leszek
The Alienation of Reason: A History of Positivistic Thought, trans. Norbert Guterman, Doubleday, Garden City, N.Y., 1968.

LEWIS, David K.
(1) *Convention: A Philosophical Study*, Harvard University Press, Cambridge, Ma., 1969.
(2) "Causation," *Journal of Philosophy*, vol. 70, 1973.

LIVINGSTON, Donald W., and KING, James T. (eds)
Hume: A Re-evaluation, Fordham University Press, New York, 1976.

MacDONALD, Margaret (ed.)
Philosophy and Analysis, Philosophical Library, New York, 1954.

McINTYRE, Jane L.
"Is Hume's Self Consistent?" *McGill Hume Studies*, Austin Hill Press, San Diego, 1979, p. 82.

MACKIE, J. L.
(1) "Causes and Conditions," *American Philosophical Quarterly*, vol. ii, 1965.
(2) *The Cement of the Universe*, Oxford University Press, 1974.
(3) *Ethics: Inventing Right and Wrong*, Penguin, Harmondsworth, 1977.
(4) *Hume's Moral Theory*, Routledge & Kegan Paul, London, 1980.

MacNABB, D. G. C.
David Hume: His Theory of Knowledge and Morality, Blackwell, Oxford, 1966.

MILL, J. S.
A System of Logic, Harper & Brothers, New York, 1859.

MOSSNER, Ernest Campbell
The Life of David Hume, Oxford University Press, 1970.

NOXON, James
Hume's Philosophical Development, Oxford University Press, 1973.

NOZICK, R.
Philosophical Explanations, Harvard University Press, Cambridge, Mass., 1981.

PASSMORE, J. A.
Hume's Intentions, Cambridge University Press, 1952.

PATTEN, S. C.
"Hume's Bundles, Self-Consciousness, and Kant," *Hume Studies*, vol. 2, 1976.

PEARS, David
(1) "Hume on Personal Identity," in *David Hume: A Symposium* (ed. David Pears), Macmillan, London, 1963.
(2) *Questions in the Philosophy of Mind*, Duckworth, London, 1975.

PENELHUM, Terence
(1) "Hume on Personal Identity," in Chappell (ed.), *Hume*, Doubleday, New York, 1966.
(2) *Hume*, St Martin's Press, New York, 1975.

Bibliography

PIKE, Nelson
"Hume's Bundle Theory of the Self: A Limited Defense," *American Philosophical Quarterly*, vol. xx, 1967.

POPKIN, Richard H.
(1) "David Hume: His Pyrrhonism and his Critique of Pyrrhonism," in Chappell (ed), *Hume*, Doubleday, New York, 1966.
(2) *The History of Skepticism from Erasmus to Spinoza*, University of California Press, Berkeley, 1979.
(3) *The High Road to Pyrrhonism*, edited by Richard A. Watson and Charles E. Force, Austin Hill Press, San Diego, 1980.

PRICE, H. H.
Hume's Theory of the External World, Oxford University Press, 1963.

QUINE, W. V.
(1) "Two Dogmas of Empiricism," in *From a Logical Point of View*, Harvard University Press, Cambridge, Ma., 1953.
(2) "epistemology Naturalized," in *Ontological Relativity and Other Essays*, Columbia University Press, New York, 1969.

RAPHAEL, D. D.
British Moralists, 1650–1800, 2 vols, Clarendon Press, Oxford, 1969.

REID, Thomas
(1) *Essays on the Intellectual Powers of Man*, MIT Press, Cambridge, Ma., 1969.
(2) *Essays on the Active Powers of the Human Mind*, MIT Press, Cambridge, Ma., 1969.

RICHARDS, Thomas
"Hume's Two Definitions of 'Cause'," in Chappell (ed.), *Hume*, Doubleday, New York, 1966.

ROBINSON, J. A.
(1) "Hume's Two Definitions of 'Cause'," in Chappell (ed.), *Hume*, Doubleday, New York, 1966.
(2) "Hume's Two Definitions of 'Cause' Reconsidered," in Chappell (ed.), *Hume*, Doubleday, New York, 1966.

ROBISON, Wade L.
"Hume on Personal Identity," *Journal of the History of Philosophy*, vol. 12, 1974.

SEXTUS EMPIRICUS
Outlines of Pyrrhonism, trans. R. G. Bury, Harvard University Press, Cambridge, Ma., 1933.

SIDGWICK, Henry
The Methods of Ethics, 5th edn, Macmillan, London, 1893.

SKYRMS, Brian
(1) *Choice and Chance*, 2nd edn, Dickenson, Encino, California, 1975.
(2) *Causal Necessity*, Yale University Press, New Haven, 1980.

SMITH, Norman Kemp
(1) "The Naturalism of Hume," I and II, *Mind*, vol. xiv, 1905.
(2) *The Philosophy of David Hume*, Macmillan, London, 1941.

Bibliography

STOVE, D. C.
(1) "Hume, Probability, and Induction," in Chappell (ed.), *Hume*, Doubleday, New York, 1966.
(2) *Probability and Hume's Inductive Scepticism*, Oxford University Press, 1973.

STRAWSON, P. F.
Introduction to Logical Theory, Methuen, London, 1952.

STROUD, Barry
Hume, Routledge & Kegan Paul, London, 1977.

UNIVERSITY OF CALIFORNIA ASSOCIATES
"The Freedom of the Will," in H. Feigl and W. Sellers, *Readings in Philosophical Analysis*, Appleton-Century-Crofts, New York, 1949.

WILL, F. L.
"Will the Future be Like the Past?" in *Logic and Language, Second Series*, ed. A. Flew, Blackwell, Oxford, 1953.

WITTGENSTEIN, Ludwig
Philosophical Investigations (trans. G. E. M. Anscombe), Blackwell, Oxford, 1953.

WOLFF, Robert Paul
"Hume's Theory of Mental Activity," in Chappell (1), *Hume*, Doubleday, New York, 1966.

INDEX

Abstract, 9–10, 152–3
actions: cause of, reasoning as, 111–12; morals and, 129–30, 136–7, 139–41
ancient philosophy, 83–4, 8–91, 148
Ardal, P. S., 181
associational laws: applied to ideas, 3, 55; applied to passiors, 109
associationism: and morals, 142–3, 145; and personal identity, 99, 100–1, 102
Ayer, A. J., 172

Basson, A. H., 181
Bayle, Pierre, 25–7, 173
Beck, L. W., 183
Beauchamp, T. L., and Rosenberg, A., 154, 185
belief: change in, and the passions, 120–1; of falsehoods, 64–9, 73–9, 82–6, 99–100, 105–6, 115–16; Hume's theory of, 6–7, 12, 21–3, 53–62, 90, 92, 146, 150
Berkeley, George, 76–8, 87, 90, 107
British Empiricism, Hume and, 1–2, 2–3
Brown, Thomas, 168–9, 185

Cambridge Platonists, 131, 135
Capaldi, Nicholas, 173
causality, 38–52, 96–7, 148, 150; and belief, 56–8, 84, 91–2; definition, 167–71; and double existence theory, 81–2, 88; and the mind, 102–4; and morals, 133–5, 141; and reasoning, 15–16, 21, 111, 116, 152
cause: definition, 39–40, 50; reason as a kind of, 15–16, 111; reasoning concerning, 21, 90, 96, 152–3; relation to effect, 41–52, 167–9
Clarke, Samuel, Sidgwick on, 131–2
constant conjunction of cause and effect, 43, 49–50, 96–8, 153
contiguity: between cause and effect, 41, 43, 49–51, 168–9; relation of, 57–8

Dancy, Jonathan, 176
Davidson, Donald, 167, 185
deductivism, 154–7, 161–3
demonstration: a category of knowledge, 14–15; in mathematics, 31–2, 34; 36; of relations, 133–4, 135–6, 138–9, 152–3
demonstrative arguments, 153–6
determination, 40, 47, 48–9
Dialogues Concerning Natural Religion, 8, 99–100
dreams, 83

Edwards, Paul, 184
effect: reasoning concerning, 21, 96, 152–3; relation to cause, 41–52, 167–9; truth as an, 15
emotivism, 141–3, 145
empiricism in Hume's philosophy, 2–3, 8–9, 11, 54–5, 65, 78, 101, 136, 146–8

Index

Enquiry Concerning Human Understanding, An, 3–4, 5–6, 8, 23, 38, 45, 66, 92, 116, 180, 185
epistemology, Quine on, 147
Essays, Moral and Political, 4, 117–22, 126
ethics and skepticism, 123–4, 126–7, 140–1
existence of objects: belief in, 64, 65–71, 75–9, 82–4, 91–2; double, 81–3, 88, 90
experience: and cause and effect, 152–3; knowledge based on, 147; and the self, 101; and transition from impression to idea, 55–7, 59–61, 87, 89, 110
extension: ideas of, 95–6, 106; Bayle's skepticism concerning, 25–35

fallibilism, 163–4
falsehoods: general rules and, 63; moral beliefs as, 144, perceptions as, 64–9, 73–5, 78–9, 87–9; reason and, 113, 115–16, 131–2; unchangingness, 105–6
fictions: philosophical, 81–91, 99–100, 101–2, 105–6, 140; vulgar, 82–3, 89, 144–5
Flew, Anthony, 175
Fogelin, R. J., 183, 184, 185

Garrett, Don, 104–5, 180, 181
general rules, reliance on, 60–3
Goodman, Nelson, 170
Green and Grose, 118

Hacking, Ian, 174, 183
Harrison, Jonathan, 141–2, 182, 183
Hendel, Charles W., 175
Hume's Fork, 110, 133

ideas: analysis of, 9–11; associated with impressions, 55–8, 72–3, 84, 94; of existence, 67–70; and Hume's empiricism, 3, 54; of identity, 72–4, 101, 105; of mental substance, 94–5; and morals, 128, 139; of necessary connection, 44, 46–51; origin of, 80–2, 94–5; reality of, 30; relations of, 110–11; theory of abstract, 59
identity: personal, 93, 98–106, 108; relation of, 71–5, 85, 88
imagination: and belief, 54–9, 61–2,
69, 82–3, 85–90; minimum reached by, 28; and origin of ideas, 82–3, 89, 91; and reality of the idea, 30; and unity of individual things, 11
impressions: and morals, 128, 139; passions as, 113–14; of sensation, 103; of sense, belief and, 54–8, 67, 69, 78; of substance, 94–5; of time, 34, 72
induction, Hume's skepticism concerning, 6, 13; and causality, 38–9, 41, 44–6, 50–1; and the imagination, 53, 55–6, 62; interpretations and criticism of, 152–66
inferences from cause to effect, 41–51, 56, 133–5, 138–9, 152–4, 158–61, 165
infinite divisibility, 27–32, 35, 36
infinity: Bayle on, 26; Hume's understanding of, 17, 25, 27–8
intuition: a category of knowledge, 14–15; and moral relations, 135–6

judgments: of cause and effect, 61, 167; moral, 125–6, 128, 132–3, 137, 139, 142–3, 145; of probability, 16, 19; truth of, reason and, 113

Kahneman, Daniel, 178
Kant, Immanuel, 26, 87
Kemp Smith, Norman, 35–6, 39–40, 42
knowledge: based on experience, 141; and reason, 35, 110; reduction to probability, 14–16, 24

liberty, 124–5
logical positivism, Hume and, 7–10, 172

McIntyre, Jane L., 101, 180
Mackie, J. L., xii, 51, 143, 182, 183, 185
MacNabb, D. G. C., 180, 181
materialism and the soul, 93–7
Mathews, Gareth B., 181
meaning: criterion of, 9–10, 11; epistemology and, 147
Mill, John Stuart, 158
mind, the: and belief in existence of objects, 70, 75–7, 84–5, 88, 99–100; concepts realized inside, 26–7, 64; disposition of, 74–5; simplicity of,

193

Index

97–8, 100; theory of, 100–1, 102–3, 107–8
mind–body interaction problem, 96
minimal perceptibilia, 28–9, 32–3, 34
morality, Hume's skepticism concerning, 7, 123–4, 125–9, 132–3, 137–45
morals: and actions, 129–30, 136–7, 139–41; and passions, 129–30, 132, 136; reason and, 123–4, 125–9, 131–45
motion: cause of thought, 96–7; Zeno's paradox, 25

natural history of philosophy, Hume's, 80–92
Natural History of Religion, 8–9, 80
naturalism in Hume's philosophy, 1, 2, 9, 15–16, 20–3, 55, 60, 65, 79, 83–4, 109, 123, 146–50
necessity, 38–52; and liberty, 125
Nozick, Robert, 164–6

passions, the, 109; morals and, 129–30, 132, 136; reason and, 110–17, 120–2; reflection and, 121
Passmore, John, xi, 1, 172–3, 180
Patten, S. C., 181
Pears, David, 102, 103, 181
Penelhum, Terence, xii, 105–6, 173, 180, 181
perceptions: of the imagination, 54–7; of memory and the senses, 54–5, 64–78, 81–3, 84, 87–9; and the mind, 103–4, 106–8; and morals, 139
phenomenalism in Hume's philosophy, 68, 84, 87, 136
Pike, Nelson, 180
Popkin, Richard, xii, 148–9, 173
Port Royal Jansenists, 36
primary qualities, 89–91
priority of cause to effect, 41, 43, 49–51, 168–9
probability, 162–4; reduction 'to nothing', 14, 16–21, 24; theory of, 58–61, 155–6; uniformity view of causation and, 45
probable arguments, 153–6, 178–9, projectionist theory, 143–4, 145
psychologism, 146–7, 148
Pyrrhonism in Hume's philosophy, 2, 23, 92, 150, 164

Quine, W. V., 147–8, 184

rationalism, and morals, 127, 129–32, 135–6, 138–9
reason: and belief, 69, 115–16; Hume's skepticism concerning, 7, 13–24, 35–7, 56, 116–17, 156; and morals, 123–4, 125–9, 131–45; and the passions, 109–17, 120–2
reflection: and morals, 139–40; and the passions, 121; on Pyrrhonian arguments, 150
regularity: of moral phenomena, 124–5; view of causation, 40, 44, 46–7, 52, 60, 157, 158–60, 167–71
Reid, Thomas, 168–9, 174, 181
relations: causal, 41–51, 55–8, 102–4, 111, 133–4, 167–71, 176; contiguity, 57–8, 168–9; of ideas, 110–11; identity, 71–5, 85; moral, 134–5, 138; resemblance, 57–8, 71, 102–4, 167, 169–70
religion, Hume's philosophy and, 8–9, 80, 97–8
resemblance, relation of, 57–8, 71, 102–4, 167, 169–70
Robison, Wade L., 180

secondary qualities, 89–92, 118–19, 127
self, the, 97, 100–2; identity of, 98–106, 108; simplicity of, 98–100, 102; wholeness of, 106
senses, the, Hume's skepticism concerning, 7, 13, 64–70, 73, 77–9, 92, 106
Sextus Empiricus, 173
Sidgwick, Henry, 131–2
simplicity: of complex objects, 85–6; of the mind, 97–8, 100; of the self, 98–100, 101; of the soul, 95, 97–8, 106
skepticism in Bayle's philosophy, 25–6, 27–35
skepticism in Hume's philosophy, 1–2, 5–7, 12, 37, 94, 104–5, 109–10, 118–19, 146–51; antecedent versus consequent, 5–6, 46, 92; concerning induction, 6, 13, 38–9, 41, 44–6, 50–1, 53, 55–6, 62, 152–66; concerning morality, 7, 123–4, 125–9, 132–3, 137–45; concerning reason, 7, 13–24, 35–7, 56, 116–17,

Index

156; concerning the senses, 7, 13, 64–70, 73, 77–9, 92, 106; epistemological versus conceptual, 6, 46; theoretical versus prescriptive, 5, 16, 22, 46
Skyrms, Brian, 184
soul, the; immateriality of, 93–8; immortality of, 97–8; simplicity of, 95, 97–8, 106
space, ideas of, 25, 26–7, 32–5
Stove, D. C., xii, 154–6, 161–4, 178, 184
Strawson, P. F., 184
Stroud, Barry, xiii, 103–4, 141–2, 142–4, 157, 172, 180, 181, 183
subjectivism, 141–3, 145
substance: Hume's discussion of, 10–12, 84, 85–6, 88–9, 94; of the mind, 94–5; of the soul, 94, 96–7

time: ideas of, 25, 26–7, 32–5, 71–2; identity over, 85, 88, 101, 105

truth: epistemology and, 147; from experience, 49; natural effect of reason, 15; reason and, 113, 131–2, 138; of reason, 49; understanding and, 111
Tversky, Paul, 178

understanding, the; and belief, 61–3; concepts realized within, 26–7; and morals, 130, 132–3, 139; operations of, 110–11; and the passions, 114; skepticism and, 20–1, 55, 92
uniformity: of moral phenomena, 124–5, 127; view of causation, 139–40, 144–6, 152, 154, 158–60, 164–5

vivacity and belief, 54, 55, 56–9, 60, 78

Zeno's paradoxes, 25

For Product Safety Concerns and Information please contact our EU
representative GPSR@taylorandfrancis.com
Taylor & Francis Verlag GmbH, Kaufingerstraße 24, 80331 München, Germany

www.ingramcontent.com/pod-product-compliance
Lightning Source LLC
Chambersburg PA
CBHW052116300426
44116CB00010B/1683